FAITH, FAMILY AND LIFE'S LESSONS

Reflections of a Christian Journalist

FAITH, FAMILY AND LIFE'S LESSONS

Reflections of a Christian Journalist

LONNIE WILKEY

Lonnie Wilkey

John 16: 33

Faith, Family and Life's Lessons: Reflections of a Christian Journalist

ISBN 978-1-955295-39-0

 COURIER PUBLISHING

100 Manly Street
Greenville, South Carolina 29601
CourierPublishing.com

PUBLISHED IN THE UNITED STATES OF AMERICA

ACKNOWLEDGMENTS

This book would not be possible were it not for my wife of 43 years, Joyce, and my children — Joanna Wilkey Beasley and her husband, Matt, and sons, Eli and Parker; and Daniel Wilkey and his wife, Jill, and daughters, Clara and Melody. They have been an inspiration and encouragement to me over the years as has been my extended family.

I also want to thank everyone who has played a role in my development as a journalist. The list is long and I fear I would leave someone out. Many have gone on to heaven, but several still remain. Thank you.

This book also would not be possible if not for those I have served with on the staff of the *Baptist and Reflector* for more than three decades, and especially the current staff of Susan Dalton (now retired), David Dawson and Mary Nimmo. The Lord has blessed me with excellent co-workers. I would be remiss if I did not cite the Communications Team of the Tennessee Baptist Mission Board, led by Chris Turner, which we became a part of about 10 years ago. They have been an extension of the *B&R*.

A special thank you goes to Mike Salva of the Communications Team for his illustration on the front cover.

Thanks also to the Tennessee Baptist Mission Board where I have served for 36 years. The columns in this book are reproduced with permission of the Tennessee Baptist Mission Board.

I also want to thank the staff of Carson Springs Baptist Conference Center in Newport for "adopting" me into their family for the two-plus years I have been based in East Tennessee. They are great.

And, finally, all credit and glory for the contents of this book go to God. Without Him, I am nothing.

TABLE OF CONTENTS

PREFACE

After graduating from North Greenville College (now North Greenville University) in 1978, I attended the University of South Carolina where I earned a degree in journalism two years later. My dream was to become a sports writer for one of the daily papers (preferably in the upstate) and cover the Gamecocks (and/or Atlanta Braves). God had other plans.

My first writing job was with North Greenville in 1980 where I served part-time while working also for the *Northwest Sentinel*, then a weekly newspaper that covered Travelers Rest, Slater-Marietta and northern Greenville County. The job at North Greenville launched my denominational writing career.

A year later, John Roberts, then editor of *The Baptist Courier*, recommended me to Baptist College at Charleston (now Charleston Southern University). While I was at Baptist College, *The Baptist Courier* published an article with my byline. I was hooked.

I later accepted a position with the former Southern Baptist Convention Education Commission as director of communications. While there, I (hopefully) honed my writing skills and began writing articles for Baptist Press. I worked in the newsroom of the Southern Baptist Convention for several years, learning from skilled journalists who could have worked for any paper in the country, but used their gifts for the Lord.

In 1988, I joined the staff of the *Baptist and Reflector* and the Executive Committee of the Tennessee Baptist Convention (now Tennessee Baptist Mission Board). I served as associate editor under editor William Fletcher Allen, another South Carolinian with *Baptist*

Courier ties. He served as associate editor with John Roberts for many years before becoming editor of the state newspaper of the Maryland-Delaware state convention and later the *B&R*.

Ten years later, I was elected as editor of the *Baptist and Reflector* and have served in that role for a quarter of a century. Man, I'm old.

During my career, God has allowed me to write countless news and feature articles and personal columns and editorials. I pray that my writing brought glory and honor to God because that has always been my intent, whether I was successful or not.

Over the years I have written numerous news stories and feature stories, but the personal columns I wrote always seemed to draw the most attention. I tried to keep them real, drawing from lessons I was learning "on the job" in life as a husband, parent, layman in my local church and in my career as a writer.

This book is a collection of columns I have written. Most of them were written under the heading of "Reflections" but some are from my early days as associate editor when I wrote "An Occasional Word." A few are related to events in the nation and denomination, but the majority are columns which relate to lessons I have learned as I journeyed through life.

The lessons are dated and for the most part are printed as they ran. One lesson I learned is that a typo 30 years ago is still a typo today, so we tried to correct those and in some cases I provided an update and changed the title if it no longer was appropriate.

God has blessed me by allowing me to write for Him over the past 40 years. I have been given opportunities that I never imagined I would have. I hope you enjoy these reflections from across time. To God be the glory!

— **Lonnie Wilkey**

Introduction

A few years ago, our Tennessee Baptist Mission Board communications team gathered around a supper table at a small diner in Millington, Tenn., preparing for the opening of our annual state convention meeting. My parents, longtime members of First Baptist Church, Millington, joined us. I went around the table introducing each team member, and as soon as I said Lonnie's name, my mother, with the revered awe of meeting Honest Abe, said, "Well, Lonnie Wilkey, editor of the *Baptist and Reflector*. I've been reading your columns for years."

She knew the legend; now she had met the man.

I enthusiastically call Lonnie a legend mostly because he is, but equally because he'll hate it. I've known Lonnie for more than 20 years and I've been his supervisor for the past 10. I've learned several things about Lonnie in our time together.

Lonnie needs no supervision. I've been in the news business and been around news people for more than 35 years. Without question, Lonnie is the most conscientious, thorough, self-starting reporter I've ever worked with. I'm not sure if it is the South Carolina Gamecock in him, but he is tenacious when pursuing stories, accuracy and deadlines.

People really are a little starstruck when they meet him, even if they know him. He seemingly knows every Tennessee Baptist. Without question, Lonnie is the face — and voice — of Tennessee's 189-year-old Baptist state paper.

He will hate being called a legend because he loathes the attention and avoids the spotlight as much as possible. Lonnie is by far the most generous, humble, kind, agreeable, committed person I know. He would literally give you his burger if you were hungry (although he might draw the line at sharing his ubiquitous Route 44 Sonic half/half tea if you need a drink with which to wash it down). He doesn't do his job for attention. He does his job because he loves his work.

He is committed to stewarding the history of the *Baptist and Reflector*. Tennessee Baptists have the privilege of reading one of the oldest continuously printed papers in U.S. history. Most papers older than the *B&R's* 1835 founding were launched in New England. In fact, the *Baptist and Reflector* is 39 years older than the Tennessee Baptist Convention's 1874 founding. Lonnie sees the *Baptist and Reflector* as the thread woven through Tennessee Baptist life and recognizes that for a people to understand where they are going, they need to understand where they've been. And because of Lonnie, Tennessee Baptists 100 years from now will have a thorough record of a 36-year stretch — 26 years as editor — where Lonnie told the story of Tennessee Baptists.

Lonnie is God-called to be a journalist. Martin Luther famously said, "Work is no longer simply a job or occupation; It is a calling, a vocation. It is a summons from God. Vocation is also where the spirit sanctifies the Christian's life, not in self-centered quest for perfection but rather in humble service to the neighbor."

Without question, Lonnie telling the story of Tennessee Baptists is nothing less than a calling of "humble service to his neighbor" as much as a pastor's is to shepherding the flock God has given him to oversee. Lonnie has faithfully served God in the life purpose to which God called him while faithfully loving and serving his family.

There is so much more to Lonnie. I've only provided you a skeleton. In the columns that follow, the legend himself offers reflections, insights, lessons and remembrances that bear evidence to a life well-lived and to a people well-served. I have no doubt Lonnie will continue to write after he retires because it is the air he breathes. However, I can humbly say, it has been my great pleasure to walk with Lonnie this past decade to the finish line of his decorated career.

It has been my greater pleasure to know Lonnie and to call him my friend.

So, without further ado, I present to you Lonnie Wilkey, editor of the *Baptist and Reflector*.

— Chris Turner
Director of Communications
Tennessee Baptist Mission Board

FAITH, FAMILY AND LIFE'S LESSONS

Reflections of a Christian Journalist

A Life-Changing Experience

(Published March 27, 1991)

"**M**issions is a life-changing experience." I've written that phrase many times when reporting on various mission trips as volunteers described exhilarating experiences. And, while I never doubted the sincerity of the volunteer, I must confess I never fully understood it either.

Now I do.

After spending two weeks in the Philippines with a team of dedicated, Christian volunteer health care workers from Tennessee and other states, missions has taken on a new meaning. For the first time in my life, missions has become real. Though I have written numerous stories and interviewed many missionaries, nothing compares with actually being on the field and witnessing things for yourself.

And, after two weeks in a Third World country, I also see the world in a different light. The real world is not a nice home, two cars and a color television. The world is the stark reality that millions of people live in absolute poverty — poverty that in some ways is different from that found in the United States.

While in the Philippines I had the opportunity to examine myself and refocus on some important truths.

• *There is power in prayer.* I saw and felt what prayer could do. Not only were countless people in Tennessee praying for the health care

3

teams, so were the Filipinos themselves. In one location, the Filipinos had met each day at 4 a.m. for three months to pray for the teams. God blessed those prayers.

• *God is in control.* Going to a foreign land can be a culture shock. Add the travel time, coupled with things you just are not used to — different restroom facilities, not being able to sleep, food you're unaccustomed to and long bumpy bus rides — and it's easy to understand why you might not cope. But because God is in control, everything worked out. Few people got sick and those who did recovered in a short time. We all "survived" what we were not used to. God saw to it because He had a reason for the team being there — to meet physical needs, but more importantly, to show a positive, Christian witness in a country starving for the message of Christ.

• *There are lessons to learn.* The Filipinos did not have much by our standards, but who is to say our standards are not too high. Just because the Filipinos do not live as we do does not mean they are wrong. The Filipinos we encountered were a gentle, loving people who gave the very best they had, even doing without to make the Americans feel more at home. They also are so appreciative of things that to us seem insignificant. That's not always the case in America. We seem to always want just a little bit more.

Those are just a few of the many thoughts that occurred to me during the trip. My wish is that more Tennessee Baptists could experience those feelings for themselves. The partnership with the Philippines continues through next March. Opportunities abound over there, not only in health care, but also in evangelism and other areas.

It would be easy to not go to the Philippines. It does take a long time to get there. Jet lag can be a problem. The culture is different. But think about the trip Jesus Christ took to the Cross for us and everything pales in comparison.

Something I overheard summed up the trip for me. As we were leaving one of the clinic sites, a volunteer told a local Filipino pastor that would probably be the last time they would see each other.

The pastor just smiled, shook his head wisely, and said, "I'll see you in heaven."

That is what missions is about.

PLASTIC LAWNMOWERS
(Published July 10, 1991)

Two preschoolers are an excellent reminder that parents always have to remember they are setting examples — good or bad — for their children.

I recently was cutting grass at my house when I noticed my 2-year-old son, Daniel, following behind me with his plastic lawnmower in the path I had cut.

Two things struck me about that innocent act. One, my son already was imitating what he saw his dad do. That made me realize I have to "be on my toes" to be a good role model for him and his 5-year-old sister, Joanna.

A second thought also occurred. Try as he might, Daniel was not accomplishing anything with that small, multi-colored lawnmower. He was doing everything right. He pushed as hard as he could. He was even perspiring like his dad, but all for naught. The grass was already cut.

These two truths also apply to our Christian lives. As Christians, we must be careful about the examples we set. We may not realize it, but non-Christians are watching our moves — ready to catch us in acts that do not bring glory to the Lord's name. That, too, is an awesome responsibility to keep in mind.

And, Christians also are guilty of "pushing plastic lawnmowers." Our actions look good on the surface, but are they actually accomplishing anything?

We are obligated out of love for our children to always be the best parents we can be and to set good Christian examples for them to follow.

And, because of our love for Jesus Christ, we have that same obligation to be the best Christians we can be, striving to set an example that will draw others to Christ, not keep them away.

MOM AND POP

(Published Sept. 11, 1991)

Sunday, Sept. 8, was "Grandparents Day." It seemed to pass with little fanfare. Except for signs in card shops or if you happened to look at the calendar, you probably did not even know Grandparents Day exists.

I don't know who thought of the concept of a day to honor grandparents. It may have been the owner of a card company, but, nonetheless, I think it's a worthy idea.

I owe so much to Howard and Leila Wilkey (Mom and Pop), the only grandparents I had the privilege of knowing. I lived all of my childhood and youth with them. Mom was a wonderful Christian woman. Because my mother (a single mother) worked, Mom and I developed an extra special relationship. Mom was the person who laid the foundation that led to my decision to accept Christ as my personal Savior.

Pop also is special. He worked in construction so he was away a great deal when I was young. But on Sundays, when he should have been resting, he always seemed to find time to play catch.

After his retirement, and Mom's death 13 years ago, our relationship has continued to grow even stronger. He lives in South Carolina, but we stay in contact almost weekly. He comes to visit if it's not "too hot" or "too cold." And, until recently, there was not much this 76-year-old man couldn't do. Health problems in recent weeks have slowed him down slightly.

Pop is an ordained deacon and he and Mom helped me develop the value system I have today. That's probably why Sept. 8 had special significance for me.

The originator of Grandparents Day had a good idea, but in reality, any day can be used to remember those people who played an important role in your life.

We don't need a "day" to drop them a note or dial a phone number. We should never hesitate to let our grandparents, or other special people in our lives, know what they mean to us.

Good Christian grandparents are truly a blessing from God.

CHRISTMAS MEMORIES

(Published Dec. 18, 1991)

Christmas is a time for remembering. I recall Christmases of my childhood and how I would look with anticipation at "what I was going to get" for Christmas.

I can remember how my grandmother (Mom) loved the Christmas season with the bright red colors and the joyful sounds. I'll never forget how excited she would be on Christmas day.

I remember the countless times I was a shepherd or innkeeper during the Christmas plays at Lima Baptist Church in Travelers Rest,

S.C., where I grew up and committed my life to Christ. Each year after those plays we would pass out fruit bags in a small block building heated by a woodstove.

I look back on those days with fondness. I now enjoy seeing my children (Joanna and Daniel) experience many of those same things.

One thing my wife Joyce and I try to express to our children is why we celebrate Christmas. And, though it may be difficult for our 6-year-old daughter to totally separate the secular Christmas from the "real" Christmas, she is well aware that Christmas is when Jesus was born.

It's nice to remember Christmases past, but we must always make sure that we never forget that first Christmas almost 2,000 years ago.

That's when God sent us the greatest gift we will ever have — Jesus Christ. My Christmas wish and prayer is that more people than ever before will open their hearts to Jesus and receive that free gift of salvation which they can have by accepting Jesus Christ as Lord and Savior.

IF IT'S NOT BROKE, DON'T FIX IT
(Published Feb. 5, 1992)

As a boy growing up in South Carolina, I used to work on a farm during the summer. We had a standing joke about two of the men I used to work with. One would drive a tractor until it fell apart underneath him while the other would take the tractor apart to see why it was running.

There seemed to be no middle ground among those two veteran farmhands.

After I bought my first car — a 1967 Plymouth Fury III — I used to be concerned about every knock and rattle that I heard. I would pester Pop (my grandfather) and he would always give me the same age-old advice, "If it's not broke, don't fix it." In other words, as long as my car is running, don't worry about it.

Those words of wisdom still apply to every area of our lives.

Just because some element may seem to have a "rattle" in it, that does not mean the whole thing needs fixing. Instead, it may just need a tune up or preventative medicine.

In any case, it's best to get someone who is an "expert" to look over the problem.

As for me, I am still not much of a handyman. Usually when I try to fix something myself, I end up spending more money because I have to pay someone to "refix" what I "fixed."

That same principle also applies to our spiritual lives and even our denomination and churches. When we have a problem there, we don't need to "fix" it. We need to turn it over to the greatest "fixer upper" of all time — Jesus.

By turning our needs over to Him in prayer, He can "fix" our problems that need repairing.

MAKING MEMORIES

(Published March 3, 1993)

It snowed in Nashville last week. After learning the Baptist Center would be closed because of hazardous roads, I looked forward to going back to bed and relaxing.

Unfortunately, my two children had other ideas. Joanna, my second grader, who usually has a hard time getting up, was up before 6:30 a.m., ready to play in the snow. Daniel, my 3-year-old, slept late — until 7:15 a.m., but he woke up ready to go outside too.

So, at 8 a.m., I am out sledding and throwing snowballs. About 30 minutes later, I drug myself back into the house, tired and sore (it hurts to fall off a sled even in the snow). I took a long nap to recover. Later that day, we went out again. I really did not mind. I was doing something all parents should do.

The kids and I did more than make snowballs that day. We made memories — memories that will last a lifetime.

Worthless or Priceless?

(Published Dec. 22, 1993)

How does one determine if something is worthless or priceless? As someone has said, "Beauty lies in the eye of the beholder."

My daughter, Joanna, enjoys art. We have many of her "masterpieces" safely stored away. One, however, has a prominent place in our home.

It's a family portrait of Mom, Dad and 4-year-old Daniel. The crayon drawing also shows an angel in the sky above us. That "angel" is Joanna's brother, David, who was stillborn as a result of the umbilical cord wrapping around his neck about a week before his birth.

Though this happened before Joanna was born, she knows that she has a brother in heaven. Her mother told Joanna about him when she was old enough to understand.

I know art critics will never pound at our door wanting to buy that "portrait." To them it would be worthless. But even if they did, we would never sell because to us, that drawing by our 8-year-old daughter is priceless.

As Christmas approaches, take time to consider what's priceless in your life. And, then pause to thank God for the blessings He has given you.

After all, Christmas is when we celebrate the most priceless gift of all — God's son, Jesus Christ.

MISPLACED PRIORITIES

(Published July 13, 1994)

Have you ever heard an older person say, "I just don't know what this world is coming to?"

I look at the high priority given to athletes in our country and I'm beginning to wonder that myself. I think we all have gone a little crazy.

Just look at all the attention given to the O.J. Simpson case. Not much is being said now about two people whose lives ended tragically. All the focus is on a "hero" gone bad.

Then, there's the story of the Columbian soccer player who was killed because he inadvertently scored a goal for the wrong team in a World Cup soccer game. Probably no one felt any worse than he did, but he will never have a chance to "redeem" himself on the soccer field again.

Don't get me wrong, I'm a sports enthusiast, but where does one draw the line over being a fan or fanatical?

In the past few weeks, I have been umpiring Little League and Dixie Youth baseball tournaments. Though I have umpired for years, from tee ball to high school and college, it never ceases to amaze and disappoint me over how grown adults act over their child's baseball game.

It's so ironic. The kids act like mature adults should act while their parents, relatives and friends behave like one would expect kids to behave.

I have seen parents berate children to the point of tears because they struck out or missed an easy fly ball.

I love to win or see my team win as much as the next person, but losing a baseball or soccer game shouldn't get to the point that it is life-threatening or image shattering.

We should teach our kids to win, but just as important, we should teach them how to lose because they won't always win in life. Just ask O.J. Simpson.

Instead of stressing winning, particularly on the non-professional level, we should go back to the time-honored values of fair play and sportsmanship. By doing so, everyone can be a winner.

EXPERIENCING LIFE'S UPS AND DOWNS

(Published Oct, 12, 1994)

Life and the Wilkey house have had their ups and downs in recent weeks — literally.

Five-year-old Daniel has been learning to ride a bicycle without training wheels. And, he has the busted lip and skinned knees and elbows to prove it.

Though I wish he had not gotten hurt, it has been fun watching him learn.

Daniel is still at that age where failure did not stop him from obtaining what he wanted. Thank goodness for bike helmets. When he fell off, even if he was hurt, he would get right back on that bike and go again. Now, he's riding that bike like an old pro.

Though he doesn't understand it now, I hope he continues to handle life's "ups and downs" like he did when he was 5 years old.

It seems like the older we get, the easier it is to let life's "downs" keep us down.

Everybody, including Christians, will have some tough times in their life. Jesus did not promise us a trouble-free life because we accept Him as Lord and Savior.

What He did promise was that He would be there to "pick us up when we fall off our bikes."

GIFT OF LOVE
(Published Dec. 21, 1994)

They do not realize it yet, but Joanna and Daniel Wilkey are learning an important truth about gifts this Christmas.

Sometime in the future, they will look back on Christmas of 1994 as the year they first realized there's something more important than simply receiving presents — that it's the giver, not the gift that matters.

On Nov. 7 of this year, my mother and their grandmother, who lived in South Carolina, went home to be with the Lord.

But having only two grandchildren, whom she loved dearly and spoiled rotten whenever she could, she had already purchased or made arrangements to purchase their Christmas gifts this year.

Years from now, those gifts will be long gone. I'm sure, however, that Joanna and Daniel will not forget the love their Grandma Ruth had for them.

It's sometimes hard for children to understand that it's not the gift that counts, but rather it's the giver and the motive behind the giving. In fact, some adults probably have not learned that lesson.

Our family would gladly give back all the gifts if Grandma Ruth could be here this Christmas, but that's not to be. We are fortunate, however, that memories of her and her love will never die.

As you give gifts this year, don't do it because it's expected or because you think someone will give you something. Instead, do it out of love. The gift may not last but love lives on.

And, above all, remember what Christmas is really about. God gave us the greatest gift of all — His son, Jesus Christ — and He did it out of His love for us.

SIMPLE AS ABC

(Published Feb. 22, 1995)

My wife Joyce and I were beginning to wonder if our daughter Joanna, now 9, would ever learn her multiplication tables while she was in the third grade last year. Finally, a few gray hairs later and halfway through the fourth grade, she has.

Now, along comes Daniel and his ABCs.

Not that the 5-year-old kindergarten scholar doesn't know them. He can recite them in order with the best of them.

But asking him to name a letter when you point it out to him is a different matter.

"A" suddenly becomes "E," "R" becomes "L" and so on.

The few hairs left on my head are becoming grayer. And, Joyce, who has more patience than anyone I've ever known, also has become frustrated.

Daniel, however, has the solution.

One night during family prayer time, Daniel, in all sincerity, asked God to help him learn his ABCs and for "Mama" to have patience while he learned them.

At the tender age of 5, he knew to do something that many mature adults fail to do — turn to God when you're in trouble.

Slowly, but surely, Daniel is recognizing his letters better and Mama's patience has improved as well. Good ole Dad just stays out of the way.

I've thought of Daniel's experience as it relates to Christianity. Today we have a good number of people who know the "ABCs" of Christianity. They know all the right things — The Ten Commandments, the Lord's Prayer, they go to church regularly, and so on.

But do they put to practice what they know? Do they witness? Do they volunteer to take on assignments in the church? Do they give regularly.

As Daniel found out, it's not enough to say his ABCs, he had to recognize them. For Christians, it's not enough to know and say what's right, you have to live it through your actions.

I'm proud that Daniel has learned already that you have to turn to God. I hope he never forgets it. It's a lesson all Christians need to remember and practice. God is "Alpha and Omega" or in Daniel's case, the "A" and the "Z."

BREVITY OF LIFE

(Published May 24, 1995)

Two events have happened in recent days which have reminded me without a doubt how precious life is — and that it can be swept away in an instant.

One story had a happy ending; the other did not.

The first one involved myself and my daughter, Joanna. I was taking her to the doctor for a possible strep infection when all of a sudden, a car made a left-hand turn in front of me. There was nothing I could do because it happened so fast. As our cars collided, sending metal everywhere, my arm went out instantly to protect Joanna. Fortunately, we both had on our seatbelts and we escaped serious injury. The driver of the other car sustained more extensive injuries, but is recovering. We were all extremely blessed. Both cars were totaled in the accident.

The other incident involved two local high school students on an outing in one of our state parks. They entered an area that was off limits and before they knew it, they slipped on some rocks and were swept down a huge waterfall, killing one and seriously injuring the other.

Two events, two different endings. I know the Lord spared me and Joanna of serious injury. I shudder when I think of what could have happened.

I grieve for the girl killed in the accident and her friend who was injured as well as their families. They will have a hard time dealing with their loss.

Both incidents are reminders that life, in just a matter of seconds, can go from fun to tragedy, even death.

It also serves as a reminder that we need to be ready when death happens. If something had happened to Joanna or me, my wife and son would have had comfort in knowing we were both in heaven with our Lord. Many people don't have that comfort or assurance when loved ones die.

As Christians we need to do our part in helping to win souls for Jesus Christ, so they will be ready when death comes. We need to forget the petty things that sometimes distract us in church and get down to the business God has called us to do.

MILESTONES

(Published Oct. 4, 1995)

Se
eptember was a month of milestones for two members of the Wilkey family.

My daughter, Joanna, turned 10 years old. It is hard to imagine that a decade has passed since she was born. A great deal has happened in her life and the world during the past 10 years. She has had relatives fight in the Gulf War. Joanna has seen new life come into the world (her brother Daniel). She has experienced the death of someone she loved (her Grandma Ruth) and so much more.

Plus, she already has made the most important decision of her life — accepting Jesus Christ as her Lord and Savior.

While I have written often about Joanna and Daniel, I have been negligent in writing about the other member of the Wilkey clan — my wife Joyce.

Joyce also celebrated a milestone in September. She began the first year of the fourth decade of her life (that's a tactful and polite way of saying she turned 40).

Also, we recently celebrated our 14th wedding anniversary. And, while that is far from being any sort of record, it is an accomplishment considering all the failed marriages we see and read about every day.

God blessed me with a wonderful wife. She has the patience of Job, which some would say she really needs since she has to "put up" with me all the time.

But she has done more than simply "put up" with me. She has been a partner in my ministry as a Christian journalist.

And, though there have been some tough times over the years, we have a stronger marriage and deeper love for each other than ever before.

Together we are working hard to be the best Christian parents we can be.

Joyce and Joanna are the two most important "girls" in my life. Each is special.

Hopefully, Joanna and Daniel will remember their childhood and thank the Lord for the mother (and dad) they had. The greatest compliment Joanna could hope to receive would be, "You're just like your mother."

A QUESTION ONLY GOD CAN ANSWER

(Published Feb. 28, 1996)

I imagine all Christians have questions we want to ask God when we get to heaven. Most of these questions are theological or things in the Bible that we wish we had more details about.

Well, I have many of those, but one question I have has nothing to do with the Bible or theology per se. It has more to do with creation.

I know God has a reason for everything He created but for the life of me, I can't figure out why God created moles. So, when I get to heaven, that's one question I just have to ask.

For the past year or so, I have had a running battle of wits with a family of moles. Guess who is winning?

I have mole hills all over my yard. They tunnel and get up close to the top so they leave fresh dirt piles in the yard. I have tried everything to get rid of those pests.

I bought some small windmills because I heard the vibration would scare them away. That worked for a while. Now, that's where the moles meet for coffee breaks.

Moth balls were one of my early options. I filled the yard with moth balls. The one thing I discovered was apparently moles cannot smell.

I bought an insecticide to get rid of grubworms, their primary food source. I thought that actually worked but after two weeks they were back. Apparently they had been on vacation.

And, finally as a last resort, I listened to the advice of one of my friends who assured me chewing gum was the answer.

I saved that one for last because it did not seem plausible.

But in a moment of desperation recently, I resorted to chewing gum. I hope no one was watching as I slipped gum down into the holes. The result? Another failure. Either moles ignored it or they actually like chewing gum.

Others have told me to get a dog or cat. They will get rid of the moles. I am not too sure. We have two stray cats that frequent my front yard and I have yet to see them eating a mole sandwich.

So until I get to heaven, I guess I will just have to keep wondering why God created moles.

When the Going's Tough, Come Up for Air

(Published Aug. 14, 1996)

I have two kids who love the water. If given a choice about what to do on a family outing, Joanna and Daniel would vote for anything that includes swimming.

They definitely didn't get that from their dad. My family teases me because I'm the only one who holds my nose when I go under water.

But I do have an excuse. I wasn't around water that much as a kid. When I was, it was usually when I was fishing in a nearby river where if

I did fall down, all I had to do was stand up. The water was seldom over waist high. Though I can swim now (somewhat) I still don't like to get in water over my head.

But because the kids enjoy water so much Joyce and I decided we needed to do something to give us peace of mind when we were at a pool. We took the kids and enrolled them in swimming lessons at the YMCA.

Joanna is almost 11 so she had a head start on Daniel because over the years she had practically taught herself how to swim.

Daniel, on the other hand, though he loves the water, was not as accomplished on the finer points of staying afloat.

Because Daniel was older than some of the other kids, he was placed in the group with Joanna and a boy who already had several years of swim lessons. I wondered about the wisdom of that move but I trusted the instructor to know what he was doing. Later, Joyce and I both questioned our decision to place trust in the young swimming instructor.

Joyce nearly fainted at the end of the first day of lessons when the instructor took the three students, including Daniel, to the deep end of the pool and told them to jump in.

No problem. Joanna jumped in and began swimming as if she had done it all her life.

Daniel jumped in, went to the bottom but popped up like a cork. With a little help from the instructor, he made it to the side of the pool.

By the end of the two weeks of lessons, Daniel was actually swimming. He still has a ways to go but Joyce and I feel confident that if he were to fall in deep water, he could at least stay afloat until help arrived.

I enjoyed watching the kids swim. They were having so much fun that I forgot how much the lessons cost. Regardless I knew it was worth the cost.

Daniel would jump in and swim furiously with his head down in the water. After a few seconds, he would stop, poke his head up to get some air and then be off again.

Life is a lot like swimming. There are times when things get tough and we become immersed in what we're doing. Unfortunately, we sometimes forget to "come up for air" and have a little talk with the Lord. We get so caught up in our daily routines and stresses that we forget the going would be much easier if we let the Lord take over and guide us.

Daniel and I were with a friend of his at a "wave pool" recently and we saw a swimmer almost drown. It was scary but it was also reassuring to see the lifeguards respond to the person who finally began to breathe again with their help.

We have the greatest "lifeguard" of all times at our disposal. He's always there when we need Him. Isn't that a comforting thought?

It's Not 'Minor Surgery' When It's Me

(Published Sept. 25, 1996)

A life experience has given me a new perspective on health issues.

I recently underwent hernia surgery. To most people, this would be considered "minor surgery." In fact, I considered it as such until I needed it.

I now have a new appreciation about what is considered minor surgery. Minor surgery is that operation performed on someone else.

When you're going under the knife, no surgery is minor. No illness is minor to the one who has it. A person's health is always going to be major to that person.

I'll never forgot my first experience. I was a coward. I'll admit it. For the first time in 35 years, I was going to the hospital to have something done specifically on me.

For people who've never been in the hospital before, it is frightening when they put you on a bed and hook you up to an IV. And when they come to "put you under" (what a terrible expression), you simply have to trust God you will wake up. Well, I survived. I did wake up following the surgery, of which I have no recollection. Thank goodness.

I was the typically ill first-time patient, according to my wife Joyce. She still laughs about some of the things I supposedly said to the nurse after I woke up.

As Baptist Hospital Sunday approaches in October, I will plug Baptist Hospital (now St. Thomas Midtown in Nashville). I could not have received better treatment. I was given first-class attention.

It is important to keep things in perspective. What's minor to you or me can be major to someone else.

FAMILY TRADITIONS MORE IMPORTANT THAN A NAP
(Published Dec. 17, 1997)

For several years the Wilkey family has gone to a nearby tree farm and cut down our own Christmas tree.

This year, with the kids older and involved in more activities, Joyce had a great idea. She would buy a tree at a local food store. It would still be a "real" tree, not artificial, and it would not be time consuming. When she told me of her plan, I readily agreed. Visions of a Sunday afternoon nap danced in my head.

Two obstacles quickly appeared — 12-year-old Joanna and 8-year-old Daniel.

"It's a family tradition," Joanna told her mom. Daniel agreed with his sister. Joanna acting sentimental and Daniel agreeing with his sister are two things that normally don't happen in our household, so we relented and agreed to go to the tree farm.

So on a recent Sunday afternoon, I sacrificed my nap and off we went for our annual family adventure/tradition. Finding a tree that three Wilkeys can agree on is not easy. I learned long ago to stay out of it and let the three of them decide. I just cut the tree they tell me to.

After several minutes of walking up and down the rows of trees, Daniel learned early that it is fruitless to compete with two females who have their own idea of what the "perfect" tree looks like. He sided with me as we encouraged our loved ones to "hurry up" and decide.

After a while, when it was obvious neither one wanted to give in, we reached a compromise. Joanna would find two trees she liked and Joyce would then make the final selection.

As we trudged back to the main office, dragging our "almost perfect" tree, I was glad I sacrificed my nap. We had a great time just being with each other. I also think our family has a better understanding of what "give and take" means in a relationship. None of us should expect to or can have our own way all the time. It's a lesson, unfortunately, some children or adults never learn.

And, while purchasing a tree in a parking lot is more convenient, it cannot replace the value of making a memory. Someday Joanna and Daniel will have their own families and their own traditions, and the four of us will not be able to go and pick out a tree anymore.

Though the tradition will end, the memories we have made over the years will last throughout our lives. That's more important than a Sunday afternoon nap.

TIRED OR DISCOURAGED? REMEMBER THE CROSS

(Published March 31, 1999)

Easter is a time to celebrate one of the two greatest days on our calendar (Christmas is the other). Without the birth and then the death and resurrection of our Lord Jesus Christ, think about how hopeless and lost we would be today.

All Christians get tired and discouraged. It happens to ministers and laity alike.

During these times of discouragement and thoughts of quitting or giving up a ministry enter your mind, remember the Cross. We should praise the Lord every day that He didn't quit.

How many of us would have continued on through the adversity and anger that was directed at Him?

Jesus didn't quit because He had a divine purpose from God. He had an assigned task from His Father in heaven and He stayed with it until the end.

As Christians, we, too, have an assigned task from God. We all have special gifts that God has given us. Some are called to preach and proclaim the gospel. Others are called by God to lead worship, teach Sunday School, work with preschoolers, children, or youth. Some are called to be ushers, to serve on church committees. The list goes on. No job is more important than the other if it is what God has called you to do.

It is easy to quit when the going gets tough. It's easy to not let yourself be the target of unfounded criticism or complaints about what you are doing, or in some cases, not doing.

John 16:33 (KJV) reminds us, "… in the world ye shall have tribulation: but be of good cheer; I have overcome the world."

On Easter Sunday, as you attend church with family and friends, thank God that Jesus did not quit. Will you?

IF TECHNOLOGY IS GREAT, WHY CAN'T I DRY MY HANDS?

(Published June 2, 1999)

Have you ever stopped to think about how much technology has changed our lives?

I am typing this column on a computer — a Power Macintosh to be exact. When I joined the *Baptist and Reflector* staff 11 years ago I had a typewriter.

Then, we set type and ran it through smelly chemicals. We let the paper dry, then "cut and pasted" it on layout boards to get the paper ready for the printer the next week.

Today we can do an entire page on a computer screen, print it out on 11 x 17 paper and it is ready for the press.

Another marvel in technology has been the advance of e-mail. It is mind-boggling to think that someone in a country like Israel can e-mail me a message that I can receive and in just minutes, send that person a reply. It sure beats mail the old-fashioned way.

Not all technology, however, has been for the better. I can think of several examples of modern technology that we could do without.

First and foremost is blow dryers in public restrooms. Have you ever noticed the wording on some of the dryers? They are careful to tell us the dryers protect the environment, they save trees, they cut down on trash and they prevent disease. That is great! If they could only dry your hands, we'd have a perfect invention.

Second on my list is automated answering systems at businesses.

I'm not referring to answering machines in homes or even voice mail. I am talking about those lifeless voices that answer the phone and begin giving you options. Unfortunately, I have never had one give me the option I needed and by the time they get around to giving you a number to press for a live voice, I have already forgotten what I wanted in the first place or gotten frustrated and hung up the phone.

Change is something we will always face. Some of it will be for the best; some of it will not be.

Christians and churches are not exempt from change. Just as change occurs in the secular world, some change is necessary in churches.

The words, "we have never done it that way before" should not be carved in stone.

Change is inevitable in all facets of life except one — God's Word. His Word is a relevant today as it was 100 years ago or will be 100 years from now. God's Word does not change.

Any changes we make in our churches should be for the sole purpose of helping more people hear the Good News of Jesus Christ. If it doesn't, then the change probably is not needed.

Y2K NEARS — PRAY BUT DON'T PANIC

(Published Oct. 27, 1999)

The "Year 2000 Problem," better known as Y2K, is fast approaching. Will it bring chaos as some have predicted, or will little or nothing happen?

It all depends on who you ask.

There are people who have literally become wealthy by predicting dire things will occur. They have caused panic among some people.

Who's to say they're wrong? On the other hand, as others argue against the wild Y2K predictions, who's to say they're right?

In other words, no one except God in heaven knows, and to my knowledge, He has not told anyone.

This issue of the paper reports on Y2K. That does not mean the paper is advocating either position. We are simply informing Tennessee Baptists about the differing perspectives on what may or may not happen as the clock strikes midnight on Dec. 31, 1999.

Y2K began receiving a lot of media attention this summer. Basically, some fear that computers not programmed to recognize years ending in four digit-dates, may interpret "00" to mean 1900 and stop functioning or create major errors. For instance, some fear that there would be interruptions in utility service and food supplies.

Many Tennessee Baptist churches have held seminars or special meetings to discuss Y2K and even to make some preparations. Some Tennessee Baptist pastors have written about Y2K in newsletters.

I tend to agree with William V. Johnson, pastor of First Baptist Church, Jefferson City. He wrote: "My best guess is that Y2K will bring us next to nothing, except some tremendous yard sales on camping equipment next spring. My only real concern is that hysterical people might cause problems around the new year. I am willing to be held self-accountable for my cynicism on this matter if I am wrong, though I have profited nothing from this whole hysteria campaign."

As Y2K approaches, don't panic. It would be wise, however, to make some preparations. The Red Cross has made available a list of suggestions that are helpful and basically could apply to any disaster situation.

The best advice is to pray and remember that no matter what happens, God will be in control.

CAN'T WINNING BE ENOUGH?

(Published Nov. 17, 1999)

I love listening to sports talk shows on the radio. It is amazing how people can get so upset over winning. Yes, winning.

You no longer hear the old cliché, "It doesn't matter if you win by one point or 100 points as long as you win." No one seems to want to win by a point anymore.

Earlier this season people were not complaining because the Tennessee Titans professional football team was losing, but because they were "winning ugly."

I listened to some University of Tennessee football fans a few weeks ago who were upset that they failed to beat a team by as many points as they were predicted. And, it is not just UT fans. I've heard fans from other schools gripe about the same thing.

These days everyone is preoccupied with the BCS (Bowl Championship Series) poll. This poll ranks the top teams in the country so that supposedly at the end of the season the two best teams in the country will play to see who is number one.

Teams have been known to run up the score on opponents so they will not slip in the rankings. They not only have to win — they have to win BIG!

My reaction to those who are not happy with just winning — you could be a USC Gamecocks fan like myself.

We haven't won but once in the last 20 games and we currently have the nation's longest losing streak. I think it would be safe to say that when, not if, we win again, we won't gripe over a one-point victory.

Something has to be wrong in our society when just winning isn't enough. Somewhere along the way we have misplaced some values and priorities over what is really important in life.

It's sad that this attitude about winning in sports does not carry over into other aspects of life.

When was the last time you left a church service on Sunday morning and said: "We only had one profession of faith this week. That's not enough. We need to go win more people to the Lord."

Think about it.

Y2K or Not, Baptist Youth Praise God

(Published Jan. 12, 2000)

Ten years ago Richard Ross of Lifeway Christian Resources and Dean Finley of the North American Mission Board came up with a concept of bringing together teenagers from all across America at the end of 1999.

Their concept grew into YouthLink 2000 and received the endorsement and support of four Southern Baptist Convention entities.

When the concept was born, leaders envisioned as many as 200,000 youth coming together to praise and worship God. What a great vision. But like any great idea which will honor our Lord, Satan began tossing monkey wrenches into the machinery. The biggest monkey wrench of all proved to be the millennium bug or Y2K.

Churches that envisioned taking hundreds of youth suddenly decided it might not be safe. And, perhaps rightfully so. Leaders of those churches had to make decisions based on information they had. So, instead of 150,000 to 200,000 teenagers and youth sponsors, YouthLink drew more than 46,000 students to seven locations throughout the United States. They were linked together by satellite link to the Holy Land.

The numbers were down and the agencies stand to lose money. Satan won a brief victory when fear kept people away. But, as always happens, God won the war.

I had the privilege of attending the event in St. Louis. Like many parents, Joyce and I had to make a decision early on as to whether we would let Joanna and Daniel go. I am thankful to God that we did and that Joyce and I also attended with the youth from Tulip Grove Baptist Church, Old Hickory, as chaperones. It was truly a blessing to see so many teenagers worshiping and praising God. More than 9,000 of them said they would consider missions as a career if called by God. Another 1,200-plus professed Christ as Savior.

My children, along with thousands of others, probably will never forget where they were when the clocked ticked from 1999 to 2000. They were among an army of teens, many of them who pledged to give their lives to the work of Jesus Christ. Praise God!

CHRISTIANS MUST CHOOSE WHAT REALLY MATTERS

(Published March 8, 2000)

Whenever I get to the point that I think nothing will surprise me, all I have to do is pick up the daily newspaper.

And, after living in Tennessee nearly all my adult life, I especially should not be surprised by anything our state legislators do. Yet, last week I was.

In the same week we had a 6-year-old kill a classmate, gas prices skyrocketing and budget and TennCare crises in the state, our legislators were worried about whether the Tennessee state flag is flown right side up.

Granted that was not the only thing they did, but they spent enough time on it that it was the page one headline in the March 3 issue of *The Tennessean.*

Basically, Sen. Bob Rochelle of Lebanon introduced a bill that proposes manufacturers label the flags so there will be no confusion which side should be flown up.

According to *The Tennessean* article, Rochelle told the state senate that the Tennessee flag, with its three white stars inside a blue circle, is flown upside down about half of the time.

Now, I want the flag to be flown correctly as much as anyone, but is it really necessary that our state lawmakers take valuable time to debate the pros and cons of putting a label on a flag? There seems to be more pressing matters of concern at this time.

Perhaps this little episode is a reminder of how all of us are sometimes guilty of ignoring the big problems and focusing on the minute. We see it in business, in our homes and even in our churches.

How many marriages have split over "nitpicky" issues? How many church business meetings been spent wrangling over what color of carpet to buy?

It is hard to deal with big problems that require thought, effort and much, much prayer. At the same time, it's easy to focus on the trivial matters.

Our world today is in trouble. … Americans are more concerned about materialism and being "politically correct" than we are about what is ultimately important — the spiritual condition of our country.

Christians have to take a stand and remind people over and over that the only hope for our nation today is Jesus Christ. In today's world that will not be the popular thing to do, but we have to do it.

As Christians, let's quit focusing on the trivial and deal with what really matters — sharing the good news of Jesus Christ.

'FAMILY TREE'

(Published Feb. 7, 2001)

L ast June my grandfather (Pop) appeared to be at death's door.
Although biologically my grandfather, Pop was in the true
since of the word, my dad. As we say in South Carolina, "he raised me."
I lived in his home from the time I was born until I moved away from
home after college.

Pop survived his ordeal last summer and lived until Friday, Feb. 2,
when God finally called him home.

Through the entire process, which lasted about eight months, both
God and Pop reminded my family of some important lessons or truths.

God reminded us all that He is in control. Last summer, not a single
doctor or nurse expected my grandfather to live. Most didn't even think
he would leave the hospital alive. Yet, he did.

God also reminded us of His grace. He could have easily taken Pop
home to heaven on that day in late June. I believe God, however, wanted
to give Pop's family time to prepare for his death. Pop came from a
strong line. He had three brothers, all near age 80 or above. His dad
lived until his late 80s and his mother to her mid 90s. Until that day last
June, Pop was always active, planting his garden and even climbing on
his roof to make repairs. He was like the Energizer bunny. He just kept
going and going and going.

Pop's brush with death reminded us that he was merely mortal and
faced what all of us must face eventually. God's grace also was shown by
the fact He enabled our family to get through the final days as we saw
Pop wither away to skin and bones, unable to eat or drink.

Through the process of dying, Pop reminded us of some important
lessons that he tried to teach all of us over the years.

First, by his actions, he taught us to trust God, not man. Pop even had to re-learn that valuable lesson after he was released from the hospital last summer. He knew what the doctors said. He knew that he was not supposed to have survived that ordeal with his heart. He basically thought he was returning home to die. As a result, he laid around, did not eat and expected to die any minute.

Then, one day he got up, got dressed and began to "live" again. Pop slowly regained his strength and began to move around, first with a walker, and then a cane. Always independent, he had to do things for himself.

Pop's determination and courage was a gift from God as it reminded us how much He loves us. He allowed us to have Pop one more Thanksgiving and Christmas. Christmas 2000 will always rank as one of my favorites because of the memories I have of Pop.

Pop was a living testimony of faith and courage. Through the entire ordeal, including the reoccurrence of the problem that happened last summer, I never heard Pop question God or complain about his condition. He faced death as he faced his entire life, trusting God to get him through. Pop did not fear death because he knew where he was going — home to heaven.

My aunt, Lynn Wilkey, who along with my Uncle Bill, Pop's oldest son, led the efforts in providing care for Pop in his last days and months, wrote the following tribute to Pop entitled "Family Tree." I believe this sums up his life.

"A mighty oak has fallen in the woods.
He was not taken by the woodman's ax.
No easy victory was this stalwart giant big and tall.
'Twas not by man but time and nature made him fall.

"His head and shoulders stood above the crowd.
One of a kind, no easy match was he.
And frailer were the ones that grew beneath his shade;
Ah! But what a grand example he made.

"A large and barren space now stands where once our guardian stood.
No single thing can fill so huge a space.
Only time and love of God can heal so huge a scar,
But we can wait because we know he watches us from afar."

I will miss Pop. He was always there when I needed him most.

I have to remember what I told Joanna and Daniel, two great grandchildren who loved Pop deeply: "We're not telling Pop good-bye. We're just saying, 'We'll see you later, Pop.' "

Thanks for the wonderful memories.

WHY ME? BETTER STILL, WHY NOT ME?

(Published July 18, 2001)

In the June 27 issue I shared about my bout with colon cancer. On July 2, I had surgery to remove a malignant tumor.

The past four weeks have provided an up and down journey on the roller coaster of life. Permit me to share some observations about this particular journey. I am sure many of our readers can relate personally or know others who have gone through similar life-changing events.

QUESTIONS

Like many people, my first question was, "Why me?" Colon cancer cannot happen to Lonnie Wilkey. But after some thought and prayer I came to ask instead, "Why not me?"

Too often Christians think we are immune to the tragedies of life. That simply is not true. One of my favorite Bible verses, especially in times of distress, is John 16:33. That verse reminds us we will have tribulation in the world, but we also have the promise of Jesus Christ, "but be of good cheer, I have overcome the world."

I know many Christian stalwarts who have had health problems much more serious than my colon cancer. Because it was detected early doctors were able to remove it and I should live a normal life without the pain and struggle many cancer patients go through. I know many other Christians who have experienced one tragedy after another. They did nothing to deserve those events in their lives.

I am no different from anyone else. Just because we are Christians, does not mean we are immune from stress or hard times.

I am also convinced that God can use the tough times in our lives and our response to those situations to be a positive witness of God's love to non-believers.

POWER OF PRAYER

Within minutes of being diagnosed with a tumor, my wife, Joyce, began lifting up prayer on my behalf. Then, she telephoned our Sunday School teacher and close friend, Stacy Bell, who immediately put my name on a prayer chain at church.

The same thing happened with the Baptist Center family in Brentwood. The *B&R* staff used the Internet and other means to inform Baptists all over the state about my cancer and to ask them to intercede on my behalf through prayer. Since then, I learned I have been on the prayer lists of many churches.

When Joyce and I returned home, following the diagnosis, the first thing we did was tell Joanna and Daniel and we prayed together as a family.

PRAYER WORKS!

My wife can be very strong. She never shared with me her fear when she saw the initial x-ray of my cancer. She tried to keep my spirits up, but she admitted later she thought it looked extremely bad. My doctor's initial reaction confirmed her worst fear.

Today we are both convinced that prayer made the difference. The tumor was malignant and had to be removed, but it had not spread and was in a location where it was easily accessible to the surgeon.

Since the surgery numerous people have shared they have prayed for me and my family.

One of the most powerful times of prayer came on the Saturday before my surgery. Joanna was scheduled to leave for Baltimore on a youth mission trip with Tulip Grove Baptist Church. She was torn. She wanted to stay with her dad but she had worked hard in preparing for the trip.

I was torn because I wanted her to be close by, but I knew there was little she could do for me before or during the surgery. I also knew God had a plan for her life and that she needed to go on that mission trip.

On the day the group left, our youth minister, Alec Cort, prayed a prayer on my behalf and for Joanna. It was so meaningful for both of us. We left each other in tears, but knowing that everything was in God's hands.

WHAT'S AHEAD?

At press time on Monday, it was two weeks since the surgery. I have returned to work but because I have not healed internally I have not been able to work full days. Each day, however, is easier with the passage of time.

I have no idea what the eventual outcome will be as to radiation or chemotherapy treatments. My personal preference, of course, would be to forego any of those options, but that ultimately will be up to my doctors.

Only one thing is certain. I know without a shadow of a doubt that the same God who was with me through the diagnosis and the surgery, is the same God who will be with me through the remainder of the process.

Thank you for your prayers and continue to lift me up. Pray that God will be glorified for the healing He has already done in my life.

GOD WAS ON HIS THRONE ON SEPT. 11

(Published Sept. 19, 2001)

The events of last week still seem like a nightmare. You want to wake up and discover that the terrorist attacks on New York and Washington, D.C., did not really happen.

But when you flip on the television set or radio, you soon realize last week was not a bad dream. It was all too real.

The sight of those airplanes flying deliberately into the World Trade Center towers will forever be etched in our minds.

Our world turned upside down that day. It can only be righted through our faith and trust in God.

There are undoubtedly many in our world today who are questioning where God was during this tragedy. Non-believers and even some Christians will ask how God could have allowed this to happen. They will ask why God allowed thousands of innocent people to die a needless death.

All are valid questions. There is no one on earth, however, who can truly answer those questions. Our God is too awesome for us to comprehend.

Perhaps the best answer any of us can give was provided by chaplain Charles Baldwin who was in the Pentagon when it was struck.

Baldwin said, "At a time like this, you offer assurance that God did not cause this to happen. Evil people in the world were the ones who attacked us. Where was God? God was present with those who suffered. He was in the fire with them."

Not only was God in the fire with the victims, He has been there with all the rescue workers, our government leaders, our pastors and ministers, and, yes, He has been with each of us who has called upon His name.

In the *Experiencing God: Knowing and Doing the Will of God* study by Henry Blackaby and Claude King, Blackaby wrote about the time his 16-year-old daughter was diagnosed with cancer. He noted that through that entire experience he never questioned God's love.

Blackaby wrote, "No matter what the circumstances are, His love never changes. … The cross, the death of Jesus Christ and His resurrection are God's final, total and complete expression that He loves us. Never allow your heart to question the love of God."

It was true for Henry Blackaby and his family and it is true in the aftermath of last week's tragic events.

God still has His hand of grace and love on America. There is no doubt.

Terrorists carried out an evil act against America. I believe it could have been much worse had it not been for God's grace.

Let's face reality. America as a whole has turned from God. We live in a country where immorality abounds. We live in a country where if you mention "God" or "Christianity," the ACLU or some other organization is there to file suit because you are "trampling on their rights."

If ever a country deserved the wrath of God, America surely does. Fortunately, however, we have a God of grace who hears the prayers of His people. And there have been many Christians here in America who have been praying for this country. I believe those prayers have kept us from being wiped off the face of this earth. God is not through with us yet.

We are nowhere close to where we need to be as a country in our relationship with God, but after last week I sense more people are coming to the realization that we need God.

I cannot recall in my lifetime the numerous references made by the secular media and government leaders about trusting in God and praying for our country. I don't recall seeing so many people from all walks of life join in prayer gatherings all across this country. Americans are beginning to see, perhaps some for the first time, that the only hope America has is in God. My prayer is that this "awakening" will last.

On the day of the national tragedy, the Executive Board of the Tennessee Baptist Convention was meeting. Board president Verlon Moore cut to the heart of the matter as only he could.

He said, "It is time to quit singing 'God Bless America' and begin living a life that He can bless."

I am proud to be an American. But I am even more proud to be a Christian. Through God's grace and His love, we will persevere.

SOMETIMES, YOU JUST HAVE TO CELEBRATE LIFE

(Published Sept. 26, 2001)

With all that has gone on in the world since Sept. 11, it has been hard to focus on anything but the tragedy that occurred in New

York City and Washington, D.C., and the crisis our nation is facing.

Joy seems to have disappeared from our lives as we witnessed the unnecessary deaths of thousands of innocent people.

But sometimes you have to find something to celebrate to keep from being constantly depressed.

With all that is happening in the world today, it's easy to be a picture of "gloom and doom." God, however, never intended for His people to remain despondent.

The date of this week's issue, Sept. 26, has long been an important event on the Wilkey calendar. Sixteen years ago today, our daughter Joanna was born. Nearly four years later, God blessed us with our second child, Daniel.

Parenting today is not easy. Our children are faced with so many things that my generation did not have to deal with.

Now, with the prospect of impending war, who knows what will happen to our children's world.

Yet, the joy of being a parent outweighs the bad.

Joyce and I have been blessed to have two children who truly love the Lord and are trying to live for Him, even at this early stage of their lives.

Granted, we have had our troubles and we undoubtedly will have a few more as we walk through these teenage years. My kids and I don't always see eye to eye, but we have a love and respect for each other.

Now at age 16, Joanna has entered a new stage of life. She already has begun driving with a permit (as if I needed another reason for my hair to turn gray) and soon will be able to get her license. In two short years she will enter college. We can celebrate Sept. 26 because that is the day God entrusted us with Joanna.

Sept. 26 will also be remembered for another reason, at least for me.

Today, I have completed six weeks of chemotherapy treatments.

Last week I finished five weeks of radiation therapy.

Words cannot begin to express the feelings I have had since June 22, the day I learned I had colon cancer. It's been a roller coaster of emotions.

Since then, I have had surgery as well as radiation and chemotherapy but God has been with me every step of the way and He will continue to be with me.

Sept. 26 indeed will be a day of celebration for our family, even with all the uncertainty in the world.

I encourage everyone to take time to celebrate life. You don't need a birthday or anniversary. We can celebrate because God has given all of us another day of life.

As the song reminds us, "This is the day the Lord hath made ... I will rejoice and be glad in it."

SPARE THE ROD?

(Published Jan. 16, 2002)

A front page article in the Jan. 9 issue of *The Tennessean* caught my attention: "School board forbids paddling."

The metro Nashville board of education voted unanimously on Jan. 8 to outlaw corporal punishment in the school system.

I wish the school board in Greenville County, S.C., had thought of that in the 1970s. Or do I?

I know it may be hard to believe, but I actually had the lumber laid to my bottom end a few times in my life while in elementary and high school. I survived and hopefully am a better person because of it.

We had a physical education (gym) teacher in high school who had no reservations about paddling, though he used another term. And, he was not alone. I remember a few of the other teachers and principals who could swing a mean stick.

College football and basketball coaches today might not have problems getting athletes admitted into universities if high school coaches today followed the example of my P.E. teacher. If you played a sport, whether varsity or junior varsity, and made less than a "C," you were introduced to his "board" of education.

Times have changed but are they for the better?

I know teachers today have to be careful because of potential charges of abuse with corporal punishment. That was really not an issue 25-30 years ago. But to do away with it completely is not a good idea.

Granted, discipline needs to start at home. I would expect that most of those in our schools who need a good swat now and then do not get it at home.

Do we put our teachers at a disadvantage by abolishing corporal punishment? What are the alternatives? Do we suspend students for "minor" violations of rules when an old-fashioned paddling might accomplish the same purpose?

Our society today is handcuffing our educators. As long as guidelines for corporal punishment are in place and applied equally to everyone and it is not abused by the teacher or principal, then I think it should be left as an option.

Remember, "Spare the rod, spoil the child."

WHAT'S A CHRISTIAN MOM? ASK THE KIDS

Guest columnists: Joanna and Daniel Wilkey

(Published May 8, 2002)

Editor's Note: Mother's Day will be observed on Sunday, May 12, in honor of mothers everywhere. I have relinquished my column space to my children, Joanna, 16, and Daniel, 13, to allow them to give their perspective of what a Christian mother is and should be.

Is there such a thing as a perfect mother?

When Daniel and I think of that, we think of the TV mom on "Leave it to Beaver" who has breakfast ready every morning, a smile on her face and great hair and make-up.

Mrs. Cleaver does not describe our mom.

However, we would not trade our mom for anything. Most of the great moms we have known didn't fit that mold at all, but they have loved their kids with all their hearts and raised them well.

Good moms know how to be a friend to their kids but they also know when to draw the line. They know when to let their kids do things and when to say no.

A mom's job is full of sacrifices. We know of many times when our mom wanted a new outfit or things like that but did not buy them because we wanted a new guitar or needed braces. She loves us so much that she's willing to sacrifice so we can have what we need.

We also know that a good Christian mom should teach her kids about God, discipline them, be there for them and provide for them.

One of the most important things a mom can do is to raise her kids to have a love for God. Our mom taught us about Jesus and to know right from wrong. She also prayed for us every day.

We have never been afraid to go to our mom with anything because we know she will listen and be fair.

Our mom may not be Mrs. Cleaver, but she's what a Christian mom should be and we love her.

IF COMPUTERS ELIMINATE PAPER, WHY IS MY DESK A MESS?

(Published March 12, 2003)

When computers first became popular I often heard it said they would eventually eliminate paperwork.

Someone didn't know what they were talking about.

If computers really eliminated the need for printed copies, why can't I find out what my desk really looks like?

There are occasions when I see a nice oak-colored top, but it doesn't last long.

I am inundated with paper. When Baptist Press began emailing their daily news releases a few years ago, I thought that would help. No more pages of BP piled up in stacks. Didn't happen. I print out hard copies (sometimes two since I occasionally lose one) of every BP release I'm sent.

Add to that copies of other news services, news releases from schools and institutions, and I could literally be buried under paper.

Then stack on copies of Baptist papers from other states, denominational magazines galore and other periodicals which pass through, a small mountain is in the making. Of course, I did learn from my predecessor, Fletcher Allen, that when the stacks on the desk get too high, use the floor behind you.

Thought emails would eliminate paper? Wrong. I end up printing and keeping copies of emails which just adds to my stacks. They far outnumber the old-fashioned letters I still receive.

Several years ago, not long after we were married, Joyce did a cross stitch for me that said, "Creative clutter is better than idle neatness." That's become my motto over the years. I keep it on a bookcase in my office. I used to keep it on the desk, but the paper kept knocking it off.

Finally, once every two weeks or so, I give up and clean off my desk and file things where they belong. Then I say I'm not going to let that happen again. Next thing I know, the process has begun again.

But I really don't mind. As a journalist and editor, I love the feel of paper. Yes, you can read the emails and articles on the screen, but there is nothing like picking up a sheet of paper and watching words jump off the page.

One of my worries as an editor and journalist is that one day all books and papers will be produced and accessed only by computer. What a sad day that will be.

The stories and photos will be the same, but no computer screen can replace actually holding that paper or book in hand and reading it up close.

So while I "complain" about all the paper I deal with, it's done in jest.

I hope we will never see the day when we won't have an actual newspaper or book to pick up and hold.

And while Bibles on tape are nice, nothing beats holding God's Word in your hands and flipping through the pages to find your favorite Scripture or that verse God wants you to see at that particular moment.

As long as I can find my desk, keep the paper coming.

HAUNTING WORDS

(Published April 23, 2003)

Last week I had the privilege of participating with about 125 other Tennessee Baptists in the first Iowa Prayer Blitz.

Tennessee Baptists from all over the Volunteer State answered the call to go to Iowa to prayer walk.

At first glance, one may wonder why we need to pray for Iowa. Missions statistics from the Baptist Convention of Iowa reveal that 90 percent of Iowans claim to be Christian.

According to Ed Gregory, a former Tennessee Baptist pastor from Savannah and Memphis, who now serves as state missions director for Iowa (among many other tasks), that statistic basically refers to people who consider themselves religious.

As we all know, there is a huge difference in being religious and being a born-again Christian.

Many Iowans fall into that category of people who were "baptized" as a baby or young child, Gregory said.

If you asked many Iowans the standard questions used by faith-sharing programs such as FAITH or Evangelism Explosion, they would answer that they will go to heaven because they are good, honest, hardworking people who have a deep love and concern for family values.

They have fallen for one of Satan's favorite ploys — to deceive people into thinking that all they need to be is to "be good" and you will walk through the streets of heaven one day. That will not get you into heaven. The only way to heaven is through the blood of Jesus Christ. Once we confess our sins and allow Jesus to be Savior and Lord of our lives, we can be assured of heaven.

After talking with Gregory, it became apparent many Iowans do not have a personal relationship with Jesus.

A Tennessee Baptist from Jackson is a real-life example of why we need to help Iowans reach their state for Christ, Heather Vest grew up in Iowa and lived there for 17 years before leaving to join the Air Force upon graduation from high school.

Heather later became a Christian and when she learned Tennessee Baptists were going to her native state, she felt burdened to go and share Christ with her family and friends.

As I interviewed Heather, she said something that has haunted me ever since. There was a Methodist church within sight of her home in Colesburg, Iowa. Heather, who was raised a Catholic, was not actively involved in her faith. As she reflected on her childhood, she noted that no one from that Methodist congregation "ever invited me to church."

Can that be said of me and you? When is the last time we intentionally invited someone to come to church with us?

Heather Vest has determined that no one will ever say that about her. She has become involved in a faith-sharing program and she shares Christ often. In Iowa she did meet and share Jesus with people she grew up with. I don't know the results of all those visits or "divine appointments," but her 75-year-old grandfather is now a Christian because Heather returned to Iowa.

How many Heather Vests have we not reached because we did not take the time to invite them to church?

STANDING UP FOR JESUS MAY REQUIRE A HELMET

(Published July 28, 2004)

In one of my weaker moments I let my wife Joyce convince me that riding a bicycle would be a great form of exercise and something we could do together.

So, we ended up purchasing two new bikes to begin this grand endeavor.

Joyce wasn't satisfied with me just riding the bike. She also informed me that I needed a helmet. I balked.

First, I was "macho" enough to think I would not fall off a bike in the first place.

Second, and foremost in my mind, I knew I had several friends (or at least two in particular and Stacy Bell and Randy McIntosh know who they are) who would "make fun of me" if I wore a helmet.

Joyce's argument was valid and, as usual, made sense.

Our 15-year-old son Daniel loves to skateboard and we make him wear a helmet, much to his dismay. However, he knows he will lose his skateboard if he is caught riding without it.

And while we have the "authority" as his parents to make him wear the helmet, what are we really teaching him if we don't lead by example?

We couldn't really justify to Daniel the reasons he needed to wear a helmet while skateboarding if he saw us riding our bikes without a helmet.

In other words, we lose credibility if we don't "practice what we preach."

Christians are faced with that same dilemma each and every day as we try to follow and serve Christ in a world that doesn't understand or care.

Sad to say, many Christians (including myself) are guilty of either not practicing what we preach or remaining silent when we have an opportunity to take a stand for Jesus Christ.

It's easy to remain silent when an issue such as the lottery, business ethics or any moral issue for that matter is being debated in the workplace.

Just as I was concerned about what my friends would think if they saw me wearing a bicycle helmet, Christians are afraid to take a stand for Christ because they do not want to be ridiculed by non-Christian friends and co-workers.

We have the mindset that by remaining silent we are opposed to whatever is being debated or discussed. Not true. Silence is seen by some as an endorsement.

What's worse is that not only are we failing to speak up for truth, we are failing to walk through open doors that God provides us to share the gospel.

Taking a stand for Christ is not easy. We may be ridiculed. We may be persecuted. It is becoming increasingly evident that Americans today do not want to be reminded about God. Already we have lost some of our "privileges" in America because we have been silent too long.

Who is our model for doing what is right? Easy answer — Jesus Christ.

Jesus suffered ridicule. He suffered persecution to the point of death on the cross.

Jesus died on the cross for our sins and rose again so that all who believe in Him may have everlasting life. Jesus is our ultimate example.

What will we do as Christians as we face upcoming elections in our nation? Will we continue to remain silent on moral issues?

Will we be so concerned about being a Democrat or a Republican that we "agree" by our silence with everything the particular party does or endorses even when we feel it is in direct violation of God's Word?

As Christians we are compelled to stand up for Jesus wherever we are and regardless of the consequences. If need be, wear a helmet. It may deflect some of the stones tossed at us.

Right or Left, the Hammer Fits

(Published March 16, 2004)

I recently had the privilege of spending almost a day with some senior adults from our church (Tulip Grove Baptist in Old Hickory) as we worked on the chapel renovation at Carson Springs Baptist Conference Center in Newport.

I walked up as Billy Warren, who is in his 70s, was on his knees hammering nails into some steps. I told him I would be glad to take over but he was using a left-handed hammer.

He stopped, looked at his hammer, flipped a switch (figuratively) and handed me the hammer and told me it would now work right handed.

I took the hammer and drove in the remaining nails. Odd though, the left handed version seemed to drive them in faster and straighter than the right handed hammer. Must have been bad batteries.

That little exchange is just one small sample of the fun you can have working with senior adults. Over the years I have worked with Billy and his wife, Janice, and several other senior adult couples in the church on various missions/ministry projects.

Each time I have received a blessing beyond measure. I have even learned a few "handyman" tips along the way, although my wife has been hesitant to turn me loose in the house.

Working in ministry projects with senior adults like the Warrens, Jerry and Judy Malone, J.P. and Linda Kirkham, Bobby and Donna Cloyd, Curt and Diane Landers, Johnny and Kay Dender, Jack Lewis and others, goes beyond having fun. These men and their wives are role models for me and "younger" folks in our church. I see their love for God and willingness to serve Him and it is an inspiration.

Every church has a valuable resource in its senior adult population. Like the hammer, our churches should fit all ages.

We would do well to keep our senior adults involved and active in our churches. They have so much to offer.

KATRINA HAS REDEFINED THE WORD 'NORMAL'

(Published Sept. 14, 2005)

Having served on the staff of the *Baptist and Reflector* for 17 years, I have written my share of hurricane disaster relief stories, beginning with Hurricane Hugo which struck South Carolina in the late 1980s.

To this point, most hurricane relief stories have been the same — deaths, extensive property damage and loss, etc. To be honest, in most of the hurricane stories I have written, all I needed to do was change the name of the hurricane and the people I interviewed. Their stories were basically the same.

In previous hurricane stories, people returned to "normal" routines within a few weeks or at least a couple of months as they began to rebuild and recover from the devastation.

Hurricane Katrina has removed the word "normal" or "typical" when it comes to natural disasters and writing about hurricanes.

I have never seen or written about a hurricane that packed the wallop or took as many lives or destroyed as much property as Katrina did when she hit New Orleans and the Gulf Coast in late August.

Lives will never be back to "normal" for thousands upon thousands of residents who fled New Orleans and other areas impacted by the Category 5 storm.

In fact, thousands of people will never return "home" again as they have fled their homes with little more than the clothes on their backs and what little they could pack in a plastic bag before they left. These evacuees have no "home" to return to and very little else. Many worked in businesses that were swept away and may or may not be rebuilt.

One thing that is the same about this hurricane is the response of Tennessee Baptist Disaster Relief volunteers. Within hours after Katrina wreaked havoc in Louisiana, Mississippi and Alabama, Southern Baptist DR volunteers around the nation were mobilized to respond.

David Acres, Tennessee Baptist DR director, and other TBC Executive Board staff members were empowered by Executive Director James Porch to "do what it took" to begin ministry to Hurricane Katrina victims.

As soon as weather conditions permitted, Tennessee volunteers were on site offering not only hot meals, but were showing God's love and compassion to those affected by Katrina.

Hurricane Katrina was atypical also because it did so much damage that evacuees fled to other states in record droves, including Tennessee.

Tennessee Baptists unable to go to Louisiana and Mississippi were able to minister in extraordinary ways — and are still doing so.

Nearly three weeks after Katrina, countless work still needs to be done to assist the victims. Tennessee Baptists have joined other Southern Baptists around the nation to respond with overwhelming generosity as funds have poured into both the TBC Executive Committee and North American Mission Board.

More funds will be needed. A word of caution: So many organizations are collecting money for victims. Most are probably legitimate,
but sadly, there will be some who "scam" goodhearted people who think
they are helping the victims.

Funds given through churches to Tennessee Baptist DR will be used
the way it was intended. Count on it. Continue to give, pray and do
whatever it takes to help those affected by Hurricane Katrina. Let them
see God's love, grace and mercy through us.

CHRISTIANITY TAKES MORE THAN AN HOUR ON SUNDAY

(Published Nov. 9, 2005)

For the past six weeks or so, Joyce and I have attended high school
band competitions and football games at McGavock High School in
Nashville where our son is a member of the band.

We have seen many excellent bands this year that are characterized
by quality musicians, dedicated band directors and a strong parent base
that works behind the scenes.

Most importantly, good bands work hard to be good. In band
competitions, the program is about 10 minutes long. Yet, it takes
countless hours week after week for as much as three months to perfect
that 10-minute performance.

After the season is over, it becomes a memory as band directors
begin to prepare for next year's 10-minute program.

Contrast that to the Christian life. Being a Christian is for eternity.
Yet, how many Christians spend the time "to get better?" Too many of
us go to church a few hours a week. Being a Christian is a 24-hour-a-day,
seven days a week responsibility.

Too many of us fail to realize that those who profess to be Christians are constantly watched to see how we handle adversity, to see what "we are really like" when we are not with the "church crowd," etc. We have to be on guard to protect our Christian witness.

In addition, we need to be active in our witness and tell others about Jesus. We need to let others see Jesus in us. A lot of Christians "talk the talk" but fail to "walk the walk."

It takes more than attending worship and Sunday School once a week to be a strong Christian. It takes commitment to spend time in prayer and to study God's Word on a daily basis. It takes a determination to live a Christian life in a world that frowns upon such.

High school bands take pride in what they do and work extremely long hours to prepare for a 10-minute performance. Should Christians do any less for our Lord and Savior? We are preparing for eternity.

WHAT WOULD GOD WANT FOR CHRISTMAS?

(Published Dec. 21, 2005)

Have you ever struggled with what gift to buy someone you love for Christmas?

I have on numerous occasions. When my grandfather was alive that was something I struggled with every year. Pop had every tool you could imagine and then some.

He could only eat so many boxes of candy and cans of nuts. Someone already had bought him a weather radio. And the list of what not to buy goes on.

Put simply, Pop didn't need anything I could get him and he was perfectly happy that my family and I traveled from Tennessee to South

Carolina each year. Just being there was gift enough for him.

But because I loved him so much, I still tried to find that perfect gift for him.

Have you ever considered this question? What gift would God want from me for Christmas?

First of all, keep in mind that God doesn't need anything. He already has it all.

But our love compels us to try to find that perfect gift for the Creator of the universe who owns it all.

What would God want from each of us?

First and foremost, He wants our heart — a heart committed to loving and serving Him.

Then, how about the gift of obedience? Wouldn't it please God greatly if His children sought to obey His Word and to share His Good News with people who haven't heard?

And I imagine God would also be pleased if His children not only went to church on Sunday, but actually lived their faith Monday through Saturday as well.

In addition, I believe God would really be pleased if we truly "loved our neighbors as ourselves."

Those are just a few suggestions of what God might want from us for Christmas. There are no doubt other gifts just as appropriate.

The bottom line is for us to love God so much that we want to please Him and give Him our best at all times.

Why?

Because He gave us His best — His Son, Jesus Christ — many years ago.

LESSONS LEARNED AT TRAFFIC SCHOOL

(Published March 14, 2007)

My wife told me for years that I would get caught. She was right. Seems like I had a bad habit of approaching a stop sign, slowing down and if there is nothing coming, giving it the gas and going through the intersection. Let's face it. I'm not the only one who does it. Hmmm. I have heard that excuse from my kids. Didn't work for them, so I guess it's only fair that it doesn't work for me.

Anyway, I did not get caught for failing to stop at a stop sign. I failed to stop at a red light before turning right (the same principle applies according to the policeman who pulled me over). I couldn't argue my innocence because I was guilty, so I accepted my punishment and headed to Traffic School.

Here are a few lessons I learned.

First, failing to obey the law (whether you think it is a good law or not) is costly. By the time I paid the administrative fee and the fee for taking the class, I probably would have been better off just paying the ticket. Attending the class kept the violation off my driving record, however, which will save money in the long run. Reminds me of sin. God will forgive us but we still must pay the consequences.

Second, everyone loves to blame someone else for their predicament. It was funny sitting in the classroom, waiting for the instructor and listening to the conversations/excuses around me.

"The policeman set up at a place where the speed limit changed and I didn't slow in time."

"Who can drive only 30 miles an hour?"

The bottom line is they, like me, broke the law. As the instructor told us when she entered the classroom, "I had nothing to do with you being here tonight."

Again, many of us like to blame others when we sin, but the bottom line is God holds each of us accountable for what we do.

Third, when it comes to driving, we know less than we think we do. We had to take a "test" as we watched a safe driving video. I confess. I didn't do that well. Sometimes we, as Christians, think we already know it all when it comes to living a Christian life. The only way that is possible is to stay immersed in God's Word through Bible study and to be in constant communication with Him through prayer.

Disobedience to man's laws or God's laws has consequences. I am grateful God doesn't make me attend school every time I break His rules. He only requires my confession of my sins and He forgives. We would all be in trouble if He didn't.

Graduation — A Special Time

(Published May 23, 2007)

My wife Joyce and I, along with thousands of other parents and grandparents across Tennessee this month, will celebrate a special time with our children and grandchildren — graduation.

Our daughter Joanna graduated from North Greenville University in South Carolina in early May while our son Daniel graduated from high school this past Sunday.

Where has the time gone?

One photo in my office shows a blond-headed, innocent-faced little boy standing in the kitchen holding his backpack prior to his first day of school. Another shows our 8-year-old "tomboy" in her baseball uniform.

That 5-year-old is now 18, has a beard and (as he likes to remind us) is an adult, while that tomboy has blossomed into a pretty young woman.

While graduation is a time for rejoicing, it is also another reminder that time marches on. As parents I think we all wish down deep we could keep our kids young and innocent forever. But that is impossible.

We live in a world that has lost its innocence. It pains me to think about all that Joanna and Daniel and their generation and younger must face in the days ahead. We think the world is evil now. Like it or not, it will get worse before it gets better (when Jesus returns as He has promised).

My prayer for all graduates, including my own, is that they will find success in the years ahead in the only way success can truly be found — through Jesus Christ.

If they define success the way our world defines success — money and material possessions — they will be disappointed because they can never be satisfied. The world's standard is to always want more.

True satisfaction will be found only when we surrender our life to Christ and allow Him to be in control.

As parents, we need to remember that although our children may be in the process of going off to college, starting a career, etc., they need our support now more than ever.

I am proud of Joanna and Daniel, and I know you are proud of your grads. As you find that special graduation gift, add something to it that will last long after the gift is gone — a promise to them that a day will not go by that you do not pray for them. That may not mean much to them now, but it will one day.

Our prayers hold the key to their future.

ONE PERSON'S WEED COULD BE ANOTHER'S FLOWER

(Published July 18, 2007)

In late June I traveled to Gulfport, Miss., to report on the efforts Tennessee Baptists are making to help residents on the Gulf Coast who lost their homes to Hurricane Katrina almost two years ago.

I also did double duty as a volunteer with 24 other people from Tulip Grove Baptist Church where I am a member.

We had the opportunity to help build a home from the "ground up" for Mrs. Spencer, an 81-year-old woman who had lost everything she owned during Katrina. She was living in a small trailer on her property.

Some of us went to the job site on Sunday to check it out before beginning work on Monday. Mrs. Spencer was excited that people had arrived to begin work on her new home.

As we surveyed the site we noticed it was overgrown with high grass and weeds. We thought it would be a good idea to cut the area before we began work.

One of our volunteers, J.P. Kirkham, seemed to have brought every tool he owned with him, including a weed eater. He immediately volunteered to clear out the area where we would be working.

As he worked, several team members visited with Mrs. Spencer who was keeping an eye on J.P. As he neared her trailer, she asked the ladies to make sure he didn't cut her "flowers."

All I saw was weeds. Now, I know most men are not that knowledgeable about flowers, but the ladies in the group, including my wife Joyce, who used to be a florist, agreed with my assessment.

But we honored her wishes and kept the "flowers" around her trailer intact.

For someone who had "nothing," those weeds/flowers represented something special to her.

We should never forget that what may seem insignificant or meaningless to us may be important to someone else.

We need to continue to pray for the people of the Gulf Coast who lost everything and continue to help them rebuild. While doing so, we must share the gospel of Jesus Christ.

People are beginning to accept Christ from seeds that have been planted on the Gulf Coast by Christians who care. Let's keep spreading the truth that one who has nothing is indeed rich if he or she knows Jesus Christ as Savior.

THE DOOR TO THE CAGE HAS OPENED; LOVE NEVER ENDS

(Published Aug. 13, 2008)

One of the classic episodes of "The Andy Griffith Show" was titled "Opie the Birdman." Opie accidentally killed a mother bird with his new slingshot, leaving three "orphaned" birds.

Opie "adopted" the three birds, named them, fed them and finally placed them in a cage so the local cat could not harm them. Finally the day came when the birds were too big for the cage and Opie and Andy both knew it was time to release the birds.

Opie was fearful that he had not been a good substitute "mother" for the birds and that they would not be able to fly away and survive on their own.

Finally, after reassurance from his dad, Opie opened the cage and the birds flew away. Opie looked at the cage and commented how empty it looked. Andy agreed but noted that the trees were "full."

That story struck a nerve this past weekend at the Wilkey house.

Our "cage" is now empty although it is still cluttered with remnants of Joanna and Daniel. The two of them embarked on a new chapter in their lives last week as they moved into an apartment they are paying for with money they are earning.

While we are excited about this milestone in their lives, Joyce and I are also a bit sad. Our "babies" have grown up. None of us can keep our children small forever, though our greatest desire is to do that so we can protect them from the "big bad world in which we live."

What has happened, though, is a natural step in the maturation process we all go through.

Like Opie, I am fearful that maybe we haven't done enough to prepare them for life on their own. We are living in a world that is so different from the one in which I was reared. While we grew up in a culture more receptive to Christian and moral values, they are living in a culture that seems to care less about anything remotely Christian or morally pure. Are they ready for the challenges and dangers of life that await? Only time will tell.

We know they will face challenges and trials in the days and years ahead. We can no longer "protect" them as we could when they were children.

Many *B&R* readers can relate to our story. Others will face it in the future. We need not fear or dread it. It is a part of life.

We have to let go and let our children live their lives. God does the same thing for each of us when we become His children. He allows us to make our own decisions when it comes to serving Him.

And at times we may disappoint Him with our behavior and disobedience, but He will never stop loving us.

Joanna and Daniel enter this stage of life with three assurances. First, they are loved by God. Second, they are loved by their parents. And, third, there will not be a day that goes by that they are not prayed for.

Joyce and I know we aren't perfect parents. We made mistakes along the way, but hopefully we provided our children with a Christian foundation on which they can build their future upon. There may be times when they drift away, but we rest on the biblical promise found in Proverbs 22:6 (KJV): "Train up a child in the way he should go and when he is old, he will not depart from it."

Our love for our children will never end. We have opened the cage door so they can fly into His arms.

A Good Mother-in-law is a Blessing From God

(Published March 11, 2009)

I have heard a lot of mother-in-law jokes over the years and I have laughed at many of them.

Fortunately, I can say that my mother-in-law (Jessie Day) and I had a good relationship over the past 27-plus years. Living 350 miles away in another state probably helped in that regard.

I began reflecting on her life last week. Jessie, as she had always wanted me to call her, has been ill for the past few months and after a gallant battle, went home to be with the Lord she dearly loved on March 6, three days after she was able to celebrate her 80th birthday.

Jessie knew the end was near last week and she gathered her five children and their families together to say goodbye. That was truly a blessing. Most people never have that opportunity.

Three things have always impressed me about Jessie. She possessed three attributes every Christian should have.

First, she loved the Lord. Church was an important part of her life. There is no telling how many babies she has rocked over the years In her home church of Forestville Baptist Church.

Second, Jessie loved her family. She was not always open with her affection, but her children and grandchildren knew she loved them. She even admitted to them the night she called them in to say "good-bye" that she had not been the best at demonstrating her love.

My wife Joyce disagreed and reminded her that while she might not always have said, "I love you," she always showed them her love.

Joyce told me how her mother used to fry chicken and would always eat the "neck." Now, just for the record, you won't find the neck in a bucket of Kentucky Fried Chicken. It's probably the least desirable piece of chicken. Yet Jessie ate it (and said she liked it) so her kids could have the better pieces.

Third, Jessie had an inner strength that went above her stature. She might have been five-foot tall, but barely. Yet, this was a woman who was widowed at age 42 with five kids under the age of 16, who didn't work outside the home and did not even have a driver's license.

But she learned to drive, found a job and provided for those five children. She taught them values and a work ethic they still hold today, and, more importantly, she took them to church. In addition, all five children are still married to their first spouse. That's amazing in itself.

I have fond memories of Jessie. She could be feisty when she wanted to and you usually knew where you stood with her — one way or the other.

My only "conflict" with Jessie occurred before Joyce and I even married. I would go visit late in the afternoons. Jessie would be busy in the kitchen and I would go to the living room where the television would be on with no one watching it. Keep in mind this was pre-cable television days. We didn't get many channels to watch. One of those, which I could not get clearly where I lived, showed reruns of "Mr. Ed," which I enjoyed. I would switch the channel, not knowing Jessie would be in the kitchen, banging pans and mumbling, "How can a grown man watch a silly TV show about a talking horse?"

Joyce later told me that while she was not watching TV, she was listening to her program. After all, she grew up in the golden age of television.

I survived that "crisis" and we enjoyed a good relationship over the years. After hearing horror stories of other mothers-in-law, I came to realize how blessed I was.

Jessie will be missed but her impact on her family and friends will last several more lifetimes through her children and grandchildren. What better legacy could anyone have?

Jessie Day with her daughter, Joyce, and grandchildren Joanna and Daniel.

TABLE SCRAPS

(Published Oct. 28, 2009)

How many times have you told your kids when they left food on their plate, "You know there are starving kids in Africa who would love to have that food?"

If you didn't say those words or don't want to admit that you did, you may have heard someone who did.

No doubt, most kids roll their eyes and think, "No one, regardless of how hungry they are, would eat this."

Well, that's not true.

On my recent trip to West Africa, I witnessed kids eating table scraps — my table scraps. Talk about a humbling experience.

On at least two occasions during our travels to villages in remote areas of Mali, we stopped at restaurants. Let's keep it in context. These restaurants are not like the ones we enjoy in the United States. Some of the places we stopped had only one or two tables and the menu consisted mainly of rice and some kind of sauce.

But on both occasions, as we went to our truck to leave, we saw the restaurant owner gather the leftover food on our plates, put it in a bowl and give it to the kids congregated outside the restaurant to eat.

They were not offended by the idea of eating our scraps. They were hungry and just glad to have food.

I was overwhelmed almost to tears the first time I saw it. I thought maybe it was just a one-time occurrence, but the next day (at a different place and location) we witnessed it again.

God used those two instances to remind me of how spoiled we are in America. Can you imagine that scene playing out in our country? It wouldn't happen.

We take so much for granted in America. Yes, I know there are hungry people in the United States, but many of our poor receive government aid so they at least have something to eat. Even those without homes can receive meals at local shelters in the larger cities.

And while I don't discount there are people in the U.S. who will go to bed at night with empty stomachs, I can't rid my mind of the image of those kids in Mali, West Africa, eating our scraps.

I know that my leftovers here won't find their way to those hungry kids in Mali, but hopefully I will be reminded to never take things for granted and to not be wasteful.

God truly has blessed me beyond measure.

REAL COURAGE

(Published Jan. 12, 2010)

On Jan. 17, many Baptists will observe Sanctity of Life Sunday. Other Baptists will let the day pass without mention because abortion (just one element of the sanctity of life) is controversial.

Controversial or not, abortion is wrong. As Christians, we should not condemn girls who get pregnant outside marriage. Instead, we need to help them realize there are viable options to abortion, whether it be adoption or choosing to keep and raise your child. We can direct these young women to crisis pregnancy centers, of which we have several all across this state. Many of these centers were begun by Baptists and other Christians.

As I get older, I realize more and more every day how valuable life is and how it can be taken away without even a moment's notice. I have known too many people who have died prematurely either through accidents or through diseases such as cancer.

We should never take life for granted.

In 1957 a young woman named Ruth served as a United States Marine, stationed in Hawaii.

A native North Carolinian, she was away from her rural home for the first time in her life.

Without going into details, this young woman became pregnant. While abortions were not legal in the late 1950s, they were available.

I will never know if Ruth considered abortion or even adoption. I doubt that she did. I do know she chose to keep that baby, a son. She received her honorable discharge from the Marines and returned to live with her parents.

Ruth, who never married, raised that son to the best of her ability with the help of her two loving parents. Instead of abandoning her and her baby, they helped her as she found a career to support her and her baby.

After I learned of her story, I never fully appreciated the courage she had. Remember, having a baby out of wedlock in the 1950s was generally frowned upon in society.

It took courage and sacrifice for her to keep the baby and make sure her son was provided for to the best of her ability.

The son she bore is alive and well today and finally has come to appreciate how special and courageous his mother truly was. Who is he? You just read his latest column.

Ruth Wilkey as a Marine with her parents, Howard and Leila Wilkey.

JEREMY'S 'LEGS'

(Published April 28, 2010)

Last Saturday I joined more than 30,000 walkers and runners in the Music City Marathon and Half-Marathon.

As I neared the nine-mile mark, I finally decided that I had lost my mind. Not only was I walking 13.1 miles (and I paid money to do it), I was walking in rain, lightning and during a tornado warning.

While many who run or walk a marathon simply love the thrill of competing and the feeling of accomplishment, others have a stronger motivation.

In my case, I wanted to "prove" to myself I could do it after I passed the age of 50. In addition, I was walking with some friends and that made it fun. And we did finish despite the weather.

Others walk and run in honor of someone or a cause.

One of those who did that is a 21-year-old college student at Middle Tennessee State University in Murfreesboro — Megan McIntosh. Megan is the daughter of Randy and Lisa McIntosh. We consider them an extension of our family.

Megan has been a summer missionary through the Baptist Collegiate Ministry of the Executive Board of the Tennessee Baptist Convention and served in California last summer when four other Southern Baptist summer missionaries were seriously injured in a car accident in Montana.

Though she did not know the four young men personally, she identified with them because they were the same age and were fellow college students and summer missionaries.

One of those young men — Jeremy (last name withheld) — was a former track athlete in college. He was the most seriously injured of the four. He is in a wheelchair and is still unable to walk.

Megan became aware of a website that was established at www.jeremyslegs.com (no longer active) and decided she wanted to honor him in this year's marathon. She designed a special shirt for the event and encouraged family and friends to purchase one to support Jeremy as well. It was not a fund raiser, just a way to show support. Several of Megan's family and friends became "Jeremy's legs" for this event.

Her reason: "I wanted to honor him because it was close to home for me. It could have been me or one of my friends."

She also is supportive of Jeremy's family who are encouraging others to be Jeremy's legs and help spread the gospel of Jesus Christ as Jeremy was doing when he was seriously injured last July.

In an era when young people often are branded as selfish and subscribing to the "it's all about me" philosophy, Megan's simple desire to honor a fellow Christian is refreshing.

I am proud of her and her love for God and helping others in His name. We could all learn a lesson in obedience to our Lord from Megan.

What's more, we can all pay tribute to Jeremy by being his "legs" and sharing Christ in our own communities.

LETTING GO

(Published Nov. 3, 2010)

This coming Saturday (Nov. 6) may be one of the toughest days of my life. But it will also be one of my most happiest days as well.

Barring something unforeseen, Joanna Elizabeth Wilkey will become Mrs. Matthew Beasley on Saturday afternoon.

I imagine my friends are making bets (not that Baptists would dare gamble, of course) as to when (not if) I cry. I don't plan on giving them that satisfaction, but it could happen. If you are a dad and have ever given your daughter away in marriage, you will understand.

For 25 years, God has entrusted Joanna into the care of her mother and me. We have been through some difficult times. We have laughed together. We have cried together.

Some say there is a special bond between a daughter and her dad just like there is between mother and son.

My wife Joyce and I love both of our children with equal passion, but there does seem to be a special bond between Daniel and Joyce as there is with Joanna and me.

Joanna and I have always shared a love for sports. She was somewhat a "tomboy" growing up. She played four sports — soccer, basketball, baseball and softball.

She especially loved baseball (just like her dad) and I helped coach her when she played Dixie Youth baseball. When I wasn't her coach, I was her biggest fan.

I was in Portland the day she struck out the same boy twice in a game, making him cry, and, yes, I might be bragging a bit. On the flip side, those who did not strike out hit the ball hard so she gave up some hits and runs, but she kept trying. Joanna did not know the meaning of the word "quit." I remember when she would get hit by a pitch that was so hard I knew it hurt, but she wouldn't cry in front of the guys. She adhered to that famous line in the movie, "A League of Their Own" — "there's no crying in baseball."

Our family was there when she was baptized, when she made her "True Love Waits" commitment and her graduation from both high school and college. We have watched her grow from a shy teenage girl into a mature Christian young woman who is able to focus on her goals.

In addition to getting married, she holds down a full-time job and is working on her master's degree.

Joyce and I basically turned Joanna "loose" after she moved back to South Carolina a few years ago, but in the back of my mind, I knew I was still the main "guy" in her life. That will change on Saturday afternoon when I walk her down the aisle.

Then, that honor and distinction will belong to my future son-in-law, as it should. The Bible reminds us that a man and woman are to leave their parents and become one. That was easier to take when I left to marry Joyce. Now, I am on the other side of the fence, but I know it is the right thing to do.

I wish Joanna and Matt nothing but the best as they become man and wife. I have tried to help both of them understand they will face tough times and situations, but they can handle anything if they put God first. I am confident both of them understand and are willing to do just that.

And while I know Joyce and I will no longer be the most important earthly people in Joanna's life, I hope she knows that she will always have a mom, dad and brother who love her very much and will be there if needed.

Congratulations Matt and Joanna Beasley. May God bless your life together!

RAS, GAS STILL PRODUCE MISSIONARIES

(Published Dec. 14, 2011)

Every Lord's Day is special, but this past Sunday at Tulip Grove Baptist Church was even more so. We had a missionary speaker. That's certainly not unusual for a Southern Baptist church, especially during the Christmas season when churches all across Tennessee are promoting the Lottie Moon Christmas Offering for International Missions.

What made our speaker "special" was that he is "home grown." Because of where he serves, I cannot mention his name or place of service but he is a product of our church. He participated in Royal Ambassadors and our youth group which is very missions-minded.

As one of our former RA leaders, I was especially proud to see and hear one of our own come back to his home church as a Southern Baptist missionary and preach God's Word boldly.

He made the Lottie Moon Christmas Offering "real" to everyone in that congregation on Sunday because we could see someone who we had a connection with who is a beneficiary of not only the Lottie Moon offering but also the Cooperative Program.

Our commitment and support of missions is one that stands out about the Southern Baptist Convention. In recent years, I believe that missions education has been devalued on the national level except for, of course, Woman's Missionary Union which keeps it on the forefront.

Missions education also is still being promoted and encouraged by leaders in the Tennessee Baptist Convention. I am grateful for that.

When I see people like the young man in our church, it reinforces the importance of missions education.

RAs, GAs and other missions organizations still have an important role to play in our denomination.

When Southern Baptists no longer support and promote missions education, that will mark the beginning of the end of our denomination.

WHEN TRAGEDY COMES, 'BOW THE KNEE'

(Published Oct. 3, 2012)

L ast week 9-year-old Sam McLeod went to heaven.
Sam had no lengthy illness. He was not killed in an accident. He just had a severe headache and within 24 hours, he passed away.

That's what makes his death so hard to understand and accept.

His parents and the physicians who attended Sam did everything humanly possible. It appears Sam died of some form of meningitis.

Sam's death was so sudden and unexpected that it literally has shaken everyone who knows the family.

Sam held a special place in my heart. I never taught him in Sunday School or had him in RAs. Basically, my only contact with him was to wave or speak briefly to him on Sunday mornings as he was passing by.

But Sam was a part of my "prayer family." His dad, Danny, has been one of my prayer partners (along with Kevin Corkern and Elbert Ross) for the past four years or so. In a prayer group you share things you normally would not mention to other folks. Our prayer group is tight and over the years we have shared the good and bad with each other when it comes to things we faced individually and as families.

When Sam was having trouble with math last year in third grade, we prayed hard for him. I doubt any kid had more prayer to help learn how to multiply than Sam did.

Sam was one blessed little boy. No child could ask for more loving parents than Danny and Glenna McLeod. It is obvious that Sam and his older brother Noah did not lack for love.

When something like this happens, it is natural to ask why did such an innocent boy with his entire life ahead of him have to die so young and so unexpectedly.

We probably will never know. The only thing we can hold to is the promise that God is still in control.

Pastor Gerald Bontrager and music and worship pastor Phil Lundy did an excellent job on Sunday morning at Tulip Grove Baptist Church trying to help our church and the McLeod family through this difficult period.

The choir sang a song I had never heard before, but it is one I will not forget. The song, with words and music by Chris Machen and Mike Harland, is entitled, "Bow the Knee."

The chorus is powerful: "Bow the knee: Trust the heart of your Father when the answer goes beyond what you can see. Bow the knee: Lift your eyes toward heaven and believe the One who holds eternity. And when you don't understand the purpose of His plan, In the presence of the King, bow the knee."

In cases like this, that is all we can do. And you know what? It will suffice because God promises us that it will.

None of us will ever know why God chose to bring a handsome, blonde, 9-year-old angel to heaven at this time, but we know He has a perfect plan for all our lives.

Pray that the McLeod family and those who knew and loved Sam will not forget to just "bow the knee" when they don't know what else to do.

A Lesson From Eli

(Published Jan. 9, 2013)

Elijah David Beasley arrived into this world on Dec. 17, 2012, about four weeks or so before he was expected.

That joyous occasion of the birth of our first grandchild soon turned into a time of uncertainty and concern.

Eli, because he was so early, had numerous health-related issues. To be honest, after we saw him the day after his birth, Joyce and I never thought he would go home with his parents.

But God used Eli to remind his Pappy and Grandma of a very important truth. Don't put your trust in what the doctors might say. Put your complete faith and trust in God.

I know that I have spoken and written about faith and trust in God for years. But when you see your first grandson in less than favorable conditions, Satan places doubt in your mind.

The doctors were so pessimistic, telling us everything that could be wrong. I guess they have to prepare the family for the worst. Ultimately, however, Eli's fate was in God's hands. And, as always, God was in control.

Countless prayers began to be lifted up for Eli, and prayer made a difference.

In the four weeks since his birth, Eli has gotten stronger each day. A myriad of tests came back positive, and though he was still in the NICU, his prognosis was good. We anticipate he will soon go home with his parents, Matt and Joanna. They have already gotten to hold him and that was a blessing.

God not only heard the prayers, He answered them.

My cousin Stewart summed it up well: "I love it when doctors have to shake their heads and say, 'I don't understand it, but he is doing so well.'"

I understand it. God did it, and He deserves all the glory and credit.

God also used Eli to remind me I needed to practice what I preach (or write, in my case). My last editorial of the year dealt with sadness at Christmas and why people can still have a "Merry Christmas" even when circumstances have you down. It was written before Eli was born.

It's really easy to give advice to others. It's not as easy to follow your own advice.

On Christmas Day, though our grandson was in NICU and we still didn't know if he'd make it, I let go and trusted God completely. I was able to wish others a Merry Christmas and mean it.

I will always be indebted to the countless people who prayed for Eli, many of whom we didn't even know. It's a reminder that we should never take prayer for granted.

Gerald Harris, editor of the *Christian Index* in Georgia, sent me this word when he learned about Eli. "I appreciate you requesting prayer for your grandson. There is no greater honor than being asked to intercede for others." Amen!

I diligently pray for others, but my goal for 2013 is to become an even stronger prayer warrior. I know prayer works. And, if I ever forget, all I need to do is to look at my grandson. He's living proof. God is so good!

ELI — A YEAR LATER

(Published Dec. 18, 2013)

Last Christmas was bittersweet for the Wilkeys. On Dec. 17, our grandson, Elijah David "Eli" Wilkey, made his grand appearance into the world.

Instead of the joy we had anticipated, Eli came more than a month early and had major complications. To be honest, we didn't think we could hold him or that he would ever leave the hospital.

So on Christmas Day last year we were not feeling much joy. As grandparents we were heartbroken for our grandson, but we also hurt for Joanna and Matt.

The doctors offered little or no hope. They kept telling us everything that could be wrong even if he survived.

The only thing we could hold to was the hope offered by a baby born to a virgin in Bethlehem 2,000-plus years ago. Romans 15:4 (HCSB) reminds us: "For whatever was written in the past was written for our instruction, so that we may have hope through endurance and through the encouragement from the Scripture."

God sent His only Son, Jesus Christ, into the world so that people like us could have hope.

We also had the hope that can only come from prayer. We know that hundreds, if not thousands of people, prayed for Eli immediately after his birth and through the entire process. He spent more than three weeks in the neonatal intensive care unit before he went home. God hears prayers!

In the 12 months since his birth, Eli has done incredibly well. Not long ago, while he was in for a checkup, the doctor who knew his medical history, told Joanna that Eli was a miracle.

We already knew that. It was not easy and at times we wondered why Eli had to have such a struggle when he was born, but we never lost hope. We knew that God could work a miracle if He chose to, and He did.

We give God all the glory and honor.

We know that Eli may still experience some health issues in the future, but let's face it. That holds true for all of us.

No matter what the television preachers may tell you, life is not a bed of roses for either believers or non-believers.

Jesus tells us: "I have told you these things so that in Me you may have peace. You will have suffering in this world. Be courageous! I have conquered the world" (John 16:33, HCSB).

With that promise you can indeed have hope!

CLOSURE NEARING IN HOLLY BOBO TRAGEDY
(Published March 12, 2014)

As a journalist, I have personally covered some heart-wrenching news events, primarily resulting from natural disasters.

But one of the hardest and saddest interviews I ever conducted occurred slightly more than three years ago.

In April of 2011, Holly Bobo, a 20-year-old Decatur County nursing student, was abducted from her home. Holly was an active member of Corinth Baptist Church in Darden. By all accounts, she was a strong Christian. A talented singer, Holly had been scheduled to sing a solo at her church four days after her disappearance. She also had participated on a church mission trip to Mississippi to help with a camp for special needs children.

Her disappearance shook not only the community but the entire state.

Flyers and posters with her photo and a phone number for people to call if they had seen Holly were distributed all across Tennessee.

In late September of 2011 I traveled to Decatur County for an interview with Holly's mother, Karen Bobo. I also met her brother, Clint, and grandmother, Donna Goff.

In a column on Oct. 5, 2011, I wrote, "The purpose of the interview was not for a 'sensational' story. Rather, it was to give a glimpse into how a family's faith was helping them through the worst nightmare imaginable — the disappearance of a child."

As I talked with Karen Bobo she shared over and over how prayer was helping her family through the nightmare they lived every day. She noted they ended every day reading Scripture and saying a prayer on behalf of Holly.

For nearly three years the family has lived not knowing what happened to Holly. They have clung to the hope that she would one day be found alive. That's all they had to hold on to.

Now, it appears that evidence has been found to indicate that Holly will not return. Fox News reported March 6 that someone (name withheld) was charged with the murder and aggravated kidnapping in the case of Holly Bobo.

While this was not the outcome the family desired and had prayed for, it does begin to give the family closure.

I can't begin to imagine what Holly's parents and family have gone through the past three years. It's one thing to lose a child; it's another thing to lose a child and not know for sure what happened.

The Bobos' world was turned upside down on April 13, 2011, and, quite frankly, they will never be the same again.

At least now, hopefully, they can cling to the hope and assurance that Holly is singing in the Heavenly Choir and that one day they will be reunited with that precious girl whose life ended so early and so tragically.

LIFE HAS ITS PEAKS AND VALLEYS

(Published Feb. 25, 2015)

During last week's ice storm in Tennessee, I took a step and suddenly was looking straight up after falling flat on my back on an ice-packed street. I was unhurt except for my pride, but it was a not-so-gentle reminder that life, indeed, has its peaks and valleys.

The week before, the Wilkey family welcomed Parker Andrew Beasley into the world. Parker is our second grandson, joining his brother, Eli.

Some of our readers may remember that there were major complications with Eli's birth two years ago. Eli spent nearly a month in neonatal intensive care but God worked a miracle and Eli is a bright, active 2-year-old who now has a baby brother.

God blessed us without the drama surrounding Eli's birth. Parker arrived safe and sound and both he and our daughter Joanna are doing well (along with Eli and son-in-law Matt).

Parker's arrival is just another reminder of the miracle of birth. Sometimes we take the birth of a child for granted, but there are things that can and do happen on occasion. Just ask any parent who has lost a child at birth or has gone through a miscarriage.

But just as special as Parker's birth was (a peak moment), I was also going through a valley.

Regular readers know that longtime *Baptist and Reflector* staff member Susie Edwards has not worked for nearly two years as she has been undergoing treatments for cancer. Susie has been an amazing trooper. Despite numerous rounds of chemotherapy and radiation, Susie and her husband, Mark, have been incredible witnesses for their Lord and Savior, Jesus Christ.

Susie, through the way she has handled cancer, has positively impacted people for Christ. Instead of focusing on her own needs and hurts, she has been "Miss Sunshine" to other cancer parents and to family and friends.

But last week we received the news that Susie has been referred to hospice. Treatments have taken their toll and Susie is very weak.

Susie has been a dear friend and an ambassador not only for the *Baptist and Reflector* but for the Tennessee Baptist Convention as well. For 25-plus years, Susie has been the "voice" of the paper, the first voice people would hear when they called the office. Susie had an amazing rapport with callers. I think many who called found reasons to call again just so they could talk to their new found friend.

Parker's birth and Susie's bout with cancer are prime examples of the ups and downs or joys and heartaches that life brings.

We all face our ups and downs in life, but as an old gospel song reminds us, "the God of the mountains is the God of the valleys."

PRODIGAL CHILDREN: THE UNSPOKEN REQUESTS
(Published Dec. 2, 2015)

Every kid who has ever grown up in a Baptist church probably can repeat the story of the prodigal son found in Luke 15:11-32. It's a story that was real when Jesus told it, and it's still real today.

The issue of prodigal children as it relates to ministers and their families is told in this issue, but it goes far beyond just being a "minister's problem." Baptists love to talk about the "rowdy" preachers' kids but the fact of the matter is that the children of the deacons, the Sunday School teachers, the missions leaders and the list goes on are all alike.

I have no data to back this up, but I strongly suspect that many "unspoken" prayer requests in churches today either are for wayward children or grandchildren. They are unspoken because most people don't want the world to know they aren't perfect. They are unspoken because the sin of pride gets in the way.

I am going to be candid. I speak from experience. My wife Joyce and I dealt with a "prodigal son" for about eight years. They were some of the hardest times of our life. We love our son Daniel dearly, but at times we didn't like him. And, the feeling was mutual.

During the "worst" of those times Joyce and I felt like we were the only couple who had a prodigal son or child. We know that was not true, but it seemed like it at the time.

We would sit in Sunday School and hear a parent or two talk about how great their kids were. We sat there and remained quiet. Both Joyce and I know now that we really had nothing to be ashamed of or embarrassed about. We raised Daniel and Joanna in church and taught them right from wrong. Both children accepted Christ as their Lord and Savior.

Ultimately, our son chose to make some really bad choices, and he has dealt with the consequences of those decisions over the years. He rebelled against his parents and God.

Children aren't always going to do what their parents want them to do or think they should do. It's that simple.

When a child becomes a prodigal it doesn't mean you are a bad parent. Normally, it means the child allowed Satan to gain a stronghold in his or her life.

Ever hear of Billy Graham? I would daresay he and his wife Ruth were excellent parents. Their son Franklin, however, readily admits he was a prodigal. Look at where Franklin Graham is today. He leads a worldwide ministry (Samaritan's Purse).

So, how did we handle it?

First, We prayed. I'm convinced that God honors prayer, especially those from a mother and dad. Daniel will never fully know how many tears and prayers were lifted up for him by his parents during those turbulent years. And, it wasn't just us. Though we might have been hesitant to state it publicly, we didn't hesitate to ask people in private to pray for Daniel. We especially relied on our family and closest friends and then we extended it to include others.

Some of God's greatest prayer warriors in Tennessee and South Carolina (and other states as well) have been lifting Daniel up in prayer for years. I have participated in a Thursday morning prayer group for more than a decade. Those men who have been a part of that group have prayed countless prayers (and still are for that matter) for Daniel as have others over the years. I suspect one day in heaven people will come up to Daniel and tell him they are glad to see him because they prayed for him when he was a teenager.

Second, we relied on our faith and trust in God. That's the only thing we had to hold on to for many years. God promises, "I will never leave you or forsake you." Truthfully, we had doubts at times, but God carried us through. There were literally days we just wanted to give up. We could not have made it without Him and His grace.

As I have talked with people all over this state I know now we were not alone then and people who are dealing with it today are not alone either. Prodigal children will be among us until Jesus returns.

It's okay to admit it. It's okay to talk about it. It's okay to seek help. We did that — on all counts. I'm not going to mislead you and tell you everything will immediately turn out wonderful if you do all that. As I said before our journey lasted for years before we began to see a change in Daniel's life.

Is Daniel where he should be today? No. While he is more receptive to God than he has been in years, he still doesn't go to church as regularly as we would hope. He still makes decisions that his mother and I don't agree with, but there's truly a difference in his attitude. A few years ago I could never have written this column because I knew he would object. Yet, when I asked him if I could share his story this week, he gave his approval. That would not have happened even a year ago.

We are so indebted to God. By all accounts Daniel probably should not be alive (he was in a terrible car accident at one point), but God spared him. He moved back with us for a short while, but God blessed him with a good job and today he is a homeowner. God has poured out His amazing love and grace on our family.

So, is Daniel still a prodigal? Yes, but so am I and I daresay there's a little prodigal element in all of God's children. With a few exceptions, I doubt there is anyone who truly is where he or she needs to be in his or her relationship to God. We are all works in progress. The good news is God will not give up on us.

If you're dealing with a prodigal child or grandchild today, don't give up hope. Rely totally on God and pray and don't be ashamed to enlist others to pray as well. Shout out that prayer request in your Sunday School class or small group even if Penny Perfect's mom or grandmother is sitting beside you. Don't allow pride to rob you of the fruits of prayer.

God honors prayers from His children. Just remember, the answer will be according to His timetable and not yours.

BULLYING: NCAA TAKES ITS BALL AND LEAVES

(Published Sept. 21, 2016)

My 3-year-old grandson, Eli Beasley, is playing soccer this fall. Personally, I think he was too young to play in a league, but Pappy deferred to his parents.

Well, Eli is proving Pappy probably was right. He takes a notion to play and practice when he wants to, causing his mother a great deal of frustration. But when he decides to play, Eli tries to do what he is instructed.

In soccer, you are not supposed to use your hands (unless you're the goalie). In Eli's game last week, he didn't particularly want to play but when the coach told him he could play with his soccer ball that piqued his interest so he went onto the field.

After a few minutes, Eli realized the players on the opposing team were trying to take his ball away from him. Obeying his coaches and not touching the ball with his hands, Eli decided the best course of action to take was to sit on his ball. My daughter took a classic photo of Eli sitting on his ball while two 3-year-old opponents looked at him with the most puzzled expressions, "What do we do now?"

I give Eli credit. He didn't take his ball and go home. Hopefully, as he grows older he will realize that sitting on the ball is not really an option either. He needs to learn to work well with others.

Apparently, the NCAA has not learned to play well with others either.

Last week Baptist Press reported that the NCAA has decided to not play seven championship athletic events in North Carolina during the 2016-17 academic year because of a state law requiring individuals at public agencies to use restrooms corresponding to their biological sex.

We talk so much about the separation of church and state. Looks like now we need to talk about the separation of sports and politics.

The NCAA has no right to force a liberal agenda on a state that has the right to set its own laws (at least for now). Tami Fitzgerald, executive director of the North Carolina Values Coalition, summed it up well in the Baptist Press article released on Sept. 13: "The NCAA is punishing the state of North Carolina because it dares to stand up for the common sense notion that everyone has a right to privacy, decency and safety in bathrooms, showers and locker rooms."

In other words, the NCAA is acting worse than a 3-year-old. This organization is trying to dictate to an entire state what it should or should not do. Their job is to "police" intercollegiate sports and make sure they are run fairly and efficiently. Instead, the NCAA is being a bully. As a result, the state of North Carolina stands to lose millions of dollars from the lost revenue that these sporting events would have brought to the state. Among the games taken away are the first and second-round Division I Men's Basketball Championship games that were slated for March 17 and 19 in Greensboro.

Instead of simply saying they disagree with the state of North Carolina and expressing a desire the state will eventually change the law, the NCAA is taking its ball and leaving.

Shame on them.

But we might as well get used to it. We are going to see more instances where money will be used as a threat. "Do it our way or the money goes elsewhere." So far, the state of North Carolina has not caved in to the threat and backed off its law. Pray they stand firm.

We see it happening over and over. Individuals and businesses are already being sued for standing true to biblical convictions. It won't be long before churches will be challenged in courts for their stands. The cultural war led by Satan is gearing up for the long haul.

Are Christians and churches today really prepared for this battle? I fear they are not. Pray, pray, and pray some more. Our only hope is Jesus Christ. Now, some good news. He's all we need.

"No one is going to kick my soccer ball." — Eli Beasley

Remember America's Heroes — Our Veterans

(Published Nov. 2, 2016)

I recently saw a video that made my blood boil. Denasia Lawrence knelt while singing the national anthem prior to a Miami Heat preseason basketball game.

Lawrence said she was protesting the number of blacks that she feels have been "unjustly killed and overly criminalized." That's her opinion and that's what makes this country so great. She can express it.

I just wish that she and all these professional athletes and entertainers would find another way to do so. Despite what they say, they are disrespecting the flag of this great country and those men and women who fought and gave their lives in order that we can be free.

Some people call entertainers and athletes today "heroes." Sadly, so did I when I was a teenager. I had sports heroes. I know now they weren't really heroes. They were just men whom God blessed with tremendous physical talents and abilities.

On Nov. 11 Americans will have the opportunity to honor a special brand of hero — our veterans — as we celebrate Veterans Day.

All of us have relatives or close friends who have served in the military. Many of us have relatives who have lost their lives during wars. I encourage every Tennessee Baptist to remember that special veteran in your life, especially those who are still with us.

I have two men who come to my mind right away. One is my uncle — Bill Wilkey. Bill served in the United States Air Force for 20 years, much of it during the Vietnam War. He truly is one of my heroes. He is one of the most solid men I have ever known. He is quiet and unassuming (and he will not like that I wrote about him), but in this case, I would rather ask his forgiveness rather than his permission.

Bill is the kind of man who prefers to remain in the background. He has never sought the limelight. While in the Air Force he was an airplane mechanic. While he never piloted a plane, he no doubt was many a pilot's best friend. He kept the planes in the air.

Over the years I have learned a lot from my uncle just by watching and observing. He is one of the hardest workers I have ever known. After his Air Force career, he worked for many years on third shift in a textile mill. He would come home and work around his house and garden (during the summer), then sleep some, and begin the process again at midnight. I never saw him show disrespect for anyone, especially women and older adults. "Yes sir or no sir" was not an option for him. It was a way of life and it still comes naturally. He loves his family but he knows how to discipline when necessary (and that extended at times to his nephew who needed it). Hopefully, I have learned from him and those characteristics are engrained in me as well.

The other "hero" I want to mention is Jerry Currey, a church member and dear friend I have written about over the years. In 1966 Jerry graduated high school and went off to serve his country in Vietnam. Two weeks prior to returning home Jerry was seriously wounded in an air attack. He ended up losing his sight, a leg, and had numerous other injuries. His body was laced with shrapnel, some of which remains in his body, nearly 50 years later.

Jerry survived and with the help of his wonderful wife, Dot, he has thrived. Life has not been easy for Jerry, but he has an incredible Christian witness that has touched the lives of countless people over the years.

My uncle and Jerry Currey are just two examples. I could name others and so can every Tennessee Baptist.

The next time you see an athlete or professional entertainer disrespecting our flag, use that as a special time to remind you to pray for our veterans — our real heroes. Without them, we would not enjoy the freedoms we have.

Three of my personal heroes are my uncle Bill Wilkey, and my two aunts, Lynn Wilkey, left, and Ruby Taylor.

THE DEADLY SIN OF COMPLACENCY

(Published Nov. 9, 2016)

The *Cambridge Academic Content Dictionary* defines "complacency" as "a feeling of calm satisfaction with your own abilities or situation that prevents you from trying harder."

Complacency can apply to individuals or organizations, including the church.

I found the word "complacency" in the Bible only once in Proverbs 1:32, HCSB: "For the waywardness of the inexperienced will kill them, and the complacency of fools will destroy them." There may be other verses that actually use the word itself, but there are many verses throughout Scripture that refer to the meaning of complacency.

Christians, especially, can fall prey to the sin of complacency. Complacency — a sin? Yes, and it can negatively impact a person's individual witness and ministry and even an entire church.

Most church statistics reveal that about 80 percent, if not more, of all Southern Baptist churches are either plateaued or declining. In other words, these are churches that have become complacent. They may have been congregations that once were on fire, reaching their communities with the gospel of Jesus Christ. They were churches that cared about those who lived in their neighborhoods. They showed the love of Jesus Christ without abandon. They met needs. When that happened, God blessed in a mighty way and those churches thrived.

But somewhere along the way, those churches (filled with individuals who became complacent) also became complacent. They began to look inside the four walls instead of outside the walls.

They began to care more about appearance and perception of the church. People began to move away from the neighborhood and those who moved in were "not like us." Over time, the churches stopped reaching out to the community. As time passed, attendance and membership decreased drastically. Some churches survived because "they had money in the bank." God does not want His people and His churches to "survive." He wants us to thrive.

Stories like these are repeated over and over in Tennessee. We have churches that are either on life support or are dead and don't know it. If you are wondering where your church falls within the spectrum, consider these questions.

When was the last time your church baptized anyone? If it's been a year or more, there probably is a serious problem.

When was the last time your church baptized anyone other than a child or grandchild of a current member? If it's been a long time, then there probably is a problem.

When was the last time your church has had visitors on a regular basis, not just during the major holidays? Better yet, when was the last time you, as an individual church member, invited anyone to church?

Tough questions, no doubt. That's why there are so many churches in Tennessee that need to be revitalized. It's no shame for churches to seek to be revitalized. It's also no shame for Christians to want to be revitalized. Revitalization is the cure for complacency.

This issue contains articles on church revitalization. Read them. They are stories of churches that finally realized they were dying and if things did not change soon, their church doors would close forever. They recognized their complacency and took steps to change and are once again making a difference in their communities.

Those are stories that can be repeated over and over, but sadly may not be. Too many churches bury their collective heads in the sand and refuse to admit they are dying. That is tragic because, in most cases, churches don't have to die. There are usually ways the ministry of a church can be saved — either through revitalization from within, merger with another church, or assimilation by another church.

Revitalization is not always easy because it involves changing from the complacency mode to once again being on fire for Jesus Christ.

God does not like complacency. Revelation 3:16 (HCSB) reminds us: "So because you are lukewarm, and neither hot nor cold, I am going to vomit you out of My mouth."

That's not a pleasant picture or thought. God does not want His people to be cold or lukewarm. He wants us to be on fire for Him.

A LAYMAN WHO MODELED DISCIPLESHIP

(Published Dec. 6, 2017)

Earl "Butch" Duty died in November.

Unless you are a member of Tulip Grove Baptist Church in Old Hickory or a lifelong resident of the Donelson-Hermitage-Old Hickory-Mount Juliet area, you've probably never heard of him.

He would likely have referred to himself as "just a layman." Butch was much more than "just a layman." He was a Christian who modeled what it meant to be a disciple of Christ.

When my wife Joyce and I moved to Tennessee 35 years ago we began attending Tulip Grove, then a small, struggling church located near Andrew Jackson's home, The Hermitage. If you drive by there now, it's hard to imagine that church was ever isolated, bordered by a cemetery and woods. The cemetery is still there but the community has grown at an amazing rate. It is no longer "country."

Some of the first people we met were Butch and Corrie Duty. Butch was our Sunday School teacher. Joyce and I had been married about a year when we began attending Tulip Grove and we were just learning how "to do church" as a married couple. Butch and Corrie took us under their wing and we learned from their example.

At about the same time we arrived on the scene, Tulip Grove called Ken Clayton as pastor. Now retired from the church (but still pastoring at Pine Eden Baptist Church in Crossville), Bro. Ken introduced the church to discipleship and evangelism. He began teaching his flock how to share their testimony and to witness. He multiplied himself by teaching a few people who in turn taught others (discipleship in a nutshell).

Among his first "disciples" were Butch and Corrie. Later, Butch took on the difficult task of discipling me. He probably looked at me later on in life and wondered where he "failed," but Butch taught me more than he could ever have imagined. He modeled what it meant to be a Christian layman active in the local church.

I remember going with Butch to visit on Monday nights. Butch had the kind of easy-going personality that enabled him to talk to anyone regardless of who they were, social class, etc. I didn't have to worry when giving my testimony or asking questions. I knew that if I stumbled Butch would step in and take up right where I left off.

Butch engaged in "gospel conversations" before that was what they were called. As far as he was concerned he was just talking with people, but he knew exactly when to just listen and when to bring Christ into the conversation.

Over the years Butch held just about every position you could have in a church. He never sought any position. The position always sought him. Butch loved the Lord and just wanted to be a servant.

One of his favorite duties for many years was heading up the men's breakfast at Tulip Grove. He pulled together three or four men and enlisted them to help. I was blessed to be part of that group. Everyone he brought in to help is still cooking today (Fred Huggins, James Lewis (since deceased) and myself) and he groomed someone (Fred) to lead after he had to step down due to health reasons, who then brought Elbert Ross into the group. That's the essence of discipleship in a unique sense.

Some of my best memories of Butch come out of those monthly men's breakfasts. We loved to kid and "aggravate" one another. Butch could do both equally well, but he "took" the kidding as well as he dished it out.

Butch Duty is just one of countless laypersons across Tennessee who love the Lord and serve Him on a daily basis without fame or recognition. My prayer is that their tribe will increase.

Hopefully, everyone has at least one "Butch Duty" in his or her life. May we never forget to thank God for those people He has placed in our paths who took the time to disciple us when, perhaps, we didn't even know that was what they were doing.

And, what's more, maybe they didn't know that was what they were doing either.

But, when all is said and done, that's what discipleship is about — teaching others how to live for Christ either through words or example. In Butch's case, he did both. For that I am eternally grateful.

THREE ESSENTIALS FOR BEING A GOOD DAD
(Published June 13, 2018)

Father's Day is coming up on Sunday, June 17. It's a time set aside for children to honor or pay tribute to their dads.

I firmly believe that having the opportunity to be a father is one of the greatest privileges that God has ever given me. It's also one of the hardest jobs I have ever had because of the responsibility that comes with the role.

Over the past few years authors have made a lot of money writing books "for dummies" — *Football for Dummies, PCs for Dummies,* etc.

Fortunately, God wrote the original book for "dummies" — the Bible, His Holy Word. God knew before He created the world that mankind could not make it on our own. We would need a lot of help and He has given that to us through His Word.

The Bible has a lot to say about being a good parent. Joyce and I have tried to instill Christian values in our children (and both are professing Christians). The verses we have leaned on over the years are Proverbs

22:6 (KJV), which reminds us to "train up a child in the way he should go and when he is old he will not depart from it," and Ephesians 6:4 (KJV): "And, ye fathers, provoke not your children to wrath: but bring them up in the nurture and admonition of the Lord."

I know I fell short in the first part of the last verse. I have a feeling my kids would testify that I "provoked" them on many occasions. But hopefully they would also testify that I tried to "bring them up in the training and instruction of the Lord."

As I reflect on what it truly means to be a good dad, I think there are three essentials that every man needs to do in order to accomplish that goal.

Marry a great mother. Joyce has been the rock of our family. When I fell short, she stood tall. I honestly don't know how single parents do it. It took Joyce and I working as a team to parent our kids. I can't imagine doing it alone. God blessed me more than I could ever have asked for when He gave me Joyce for my wife.

Pray, pray, pray. You can't say it enough. Prayer is one of the key ingredients of being a good parent. We can't do it on our own power and strength. Parenting is hard. When we faced difficult times and didn't know what to do, we prayed. And, we asked others to pray for us and our children when needed. That's critical. Don't be so proud that you won't ask others to pray.

Turn it over to God. As parents, we are going to "mess it up." Our children will make mistakes and so will parents. We have to trust God because He ultimately is in complete control.

I'm the first to admit I am not a perfect dad. I honestly don't know if I've been a good dad. Only my kids can answer that one. But I can say that I've been a loving dad who tried to instill Christian values in his children.

As the best cooks would say, the proof is in the pudding. My children, just like me and Joyce, and everyone else for that matter, are works in progress. But I see signs that Joyce and I did "something right."

Our oldest grandson, Eli, is a miracle from God. By all accounts he should have died at birth, but God spared him. Last week, he participated in his pre-K program at school. Our daughter, Joanna, wrote these words on Facebook following the program:

"I'm so proud of this kid. At the beginning of the school year, his progress in school was a little worrisome. He ended up being diagnosed with ADHD and a sensory processing disorder. By the end of the year, he was right on track and won awards for knowing all of his letters, sounds and being able to write his name. … In a letter his teacher wrote to him, she said, 'Eli, you're a wonder!' His doctors all think so, too. It's a wonder he's alive, it's a wonder he's not severely disabled, and it's a wonder he's on track for his age. He continues to defy the odds and I'm in awe of what God has done in his life and continues to do."

That tells me she knows who's really in charge.

And, by the time the next paper is published, our son Daniel will be married to a wonderful young lady named Jill Pransky. It's no secret Daniel and I had some issues during his teenage years, but he turned his life around (and back toward God). His marriage to Jill is evidence of a life that has been changed by God's wonderful grace and mercy.

I am proud of both of my children and the adults they have become. God has truly blessed me and for that I am thankful and indebted to Him. My prayer is that every dad in Tennessee can claim that same blessing.

A Trip to Mayberry

(Published Aug. 29, 2018)

Last week my wife, Joyce, and I made my long-awaited trip to Mayberry. Actually, it was to Mount Airy, N.C. As many people know, Mayberry is the fictional North Carolina town that was home to *The Andy Griffith Show* for eight seasons.

As a kid and an adult, I have watched that show so many times I can actually carry on some of the dialogue. It's a timeless classic of simple times, long before computers, the internet, cell phones, and every other communications device known to man.

The only way to communicate in Mayberry was face-to-face conversation or hopefully that Sarah (the never-seen phone operator) could get you through to the person you needed to speak to. After all, they were on a "party line."

Mount Airy is the boyhood home of Andy Griffith. Many of the names and places used on *The Andy Griffith Show* are actual names and places in or near Mount Airy. We visited the Andy Griffith Museum and even got to meet Betty Lynn, the actress who played Thelma Lou (Barney Fife's girlfriend on the show).

While waiting in line to meet Thelma Lou and get my photo made with her and an autograph (yes, I was the typical starry-eyed tourist), I visited with other fans. Betty Lynn only signs once a month normally, so the museum had a greater number of visitors that day than I could have imagined. I stood in line with probably more than 100 people. Included among them was a family of five from Maryland. The mother was in her 40s and she had two daughters (probably about 12 and 13) and a younger son of about 8 or 9. They had been in town the entire week and had taken in all the sights, including the tour of the town in a Mayberry replica police car.

Their love for the show is amazing. None of them (the mom or dad and certainly not the kids) were even born when the show first aired in 1960. I was only 2 years old myself. But it has become an iconic show for people of all ages.

Why?

I think it is because deep down inside we yearn for the simpler times of life — where you could sit on the front porch in a rocking chair and truly relax and have meaningful conversations, a place where everybody knows everybody and they actually care for each other, a place where your kids could roam the neighborhood and you didn't have to worry about their safety.

We yearn for the "security" that small-town atmosphere provided. In those days, most families never locked their doors. You could walk down the street without fear of being robbed or mugged.

Mayberry was not perfect. Townspeople had their squabbles and fights. It had a town drunk, jaywalkers (a no-no in Barney's world), gossipers, and even a bank robbery on occasion. But in the end, everyone co-existed in harmony for the most part.

Deep down, we all want a Mayberry lifestyle whether we admit it or not. But most of us are realistic enough to know that Mayberry, after all, never really existed. But we can dream and long for such a place.

We will never find Mayberry on this earth, but I can't help but feel heaven will seem a lot like Mayberry. Andy and Barney won't be there, but Jesus will be. How better could it be than to spend eternity with Him in heaven?

If I could enjoy a trip to a town that never even existed, think how much more I will enjoy heaven — a place that is real and is for eternity.

Lonnie and Joyce Wilkey with Betty Lynn (Thelma Lou)

MAN'S BEST FRIEND

(Published July 10, 2019)

I have heard that a dog is a "man's best friend" for most of my life.

As a child growing up, dogs were not my best friends. I didn't like dogs and dogs didn't like me, as evidenced by being bitten several times by "man's best friend." Dogs were a part of God's creation that I thought I could do without.

When I became an adult, I tolerated dogs and could be around them, but never had a desire to own one. Finally, our kids, Joanna and

Daniel, prevailed and talked Mom and Dad (mainly me because Joyce was okay with it) into allowing them to have a dog. I did so, grudgingly, with the stipulation it would be an outside dog. No dogs in my house, I proclaimed.

Smoky lasted with us for a year or so before he became a safety issue (to others). He didn't like people other than us (and probably didn't like me, but at least he didn't bite me).

So, the Wilkeys have been dog free ever since, well almost. When our son Daniel lived in Austin a few years, he adopted Conway, a Catahoula breed. Or, it may have been that Conway adopted Daniel. Regardless, Conway was one of the best things that happened to Daniel while he was away from home. They needed each other.

After Daniel moved back to Tennessee, he lived with us for a brief time. So did Conway. I said Conway could stay, but he would be an outside dog. Conway had other plans. In his mind, he was an inside dog. End of story. I lost that battle before it even started. I then said he had to stay in Daniel's bedroom and couldn't roam the house. That lasted until Conway basically broke down the bedroom door. Despite being ready to send him back to Austin (with or without Daniel), I finally got used to having him around and Conway found a place in my heart.

Daniel later moved out and eventually married and Conway went along, of course. When he married our daughter-in-law Jill, her dog Lily also became a "member of the family." So, guess who gets called on to "dog sit" when they go out of town. Over the years Conway and Lily have been frequent guests, much to the dismay of Joyce's cats.

Conway and I grew closer over the years. It probably helped that he could always depend on me to "accidently" drop people food in his presence. He loved cheeseburgers and hot dogs more than I do.

When Daniel acquired Conway, he didn't know how old he was but he was not a young dog. Seven years have passed since Conway joined the family and he had to be put to sleep last week due to cancer.

I never thought I would grieve for any animal, especially a dog, but I confess that I did so when we lost Conway. Conway taught me a thing or two about loyalty and unconditional love. Conway, for the most part was gentle and never bothered anyone, unless they came on his "turf" and he felt the need to protect "his people." He loved his family and we all loved him.

I never really understood what "man's best friend" meant until Conway came along. Now I know. He will be missed.

Conway and Lily

TENNESSEE BAPTIST LIGHT SHINES AMID DARKNESS

(Published Aug. 21, 2019)

E vil is real. Don't let anyone tell you it's not.

How do we really know? "For the Bible tells me so."

Do a "Google" search on the internet and you will find a multitude of verses that proclaim evil is real. First John 5:19 leaves no doubt: "We know that we are of God, and the whole world is under the sway of the evil one" (CSB). That's about as plain as it gets.

I experienced darkness firsthand last week. Chris Turner and I attended the Tennessee Senate Judiciary Summer Study Committee on Aug. 12 to support Randy C. Davis, president and executive director of the Tennessee Baptist Mission Board. He was on the agenda as a pro-life advocate. As most Tennessee Baptists are aware, Dr. Davis initiated "I Stand for Life," an effort to mobilize Tennessee Baptists to let our state legislators know where Tennessee Baptists stand on abortion.

In just three weeks, the effort garnered more than 16,000 signatures on a petition (and several thousand more since then), along with nearly 1,000 signatures from Tennessee Baptist pastors.

Due to the large crowd (both pro-life and abortion proponents) that attended, many people were unable to stay in the room where the committee hearing was held due to the size of the crowd and fire codes. Many of us, myself included, found one of the overflow rooms. Within a few minutes, I was surrounded by dozens of Planned Parenthood supporters.

As they entered, I truly felt Satan's presence. The room was dark, not literally but figuratively. It was, without a doubt, one of the most uncomfortable meetings I have ever attended during my 32 years with the *Baptist and Reflector*.

As I heard them talk among themselves, I kept wondering how their hearts could be so hardened that they could not understand they were supporting the termination of a human life or that they simply did not care.

But Scripture once again puts it in perspective: "From their callous hearts comes iniquity; their evil imaginations have no limits" (Psalm 73:7, NIV). Facts don't matter to a hardened heart and a mind that is already made up.

We were there during the "pro-life" testimony. Abortion advocates had their time before the senate committee the following day. As speaker after speaker spoke from a pro-life perspective, it was evident the abortion advocates were not interested in "truth." They were there to be seen and to be heard. For the most part, they behaved well, but a few times, especially when our TBMB executive director spoke, they were loud with their disapproval. Though they abhor truth, it strikes a chord when heard. Tennessee Baptists have reason to be proud of their leader. Randy Davis stood tall last week as he shared the truth of God's Word. His light illuminated that room though they were oblivious.

Years ago, when I helped with Royal Ambassadors at my former church, we would take the boys on trips to caves. We would go deep inside the earth and get to a point where my friend and caving expert Steve York would have everyone turn off their flashlight. There was complete darkness. You could not see your hand in front of your face. Slowly, a light would flicker on, if only for an instant. But that was all it took — one light to penetrate the darkness.

Our world today is dark. Last week, Dr. Davis and Tennessee Baptists were gospel lights in advocating for the value of life.

Scripture reminds Christians that we "are the light of the world. ... No one lights a lamp and puts it under a basket, but rather on a lampstand, and it gives light for all who are in the house" (Matthew 5:14-15, CSB).

As darkness continues to permeate our nation, Tennessee Baptists must continue to lead the charge and be "salt and light" to a world that desperately needs Jesus Christ. The only thing that will ultimately stop abortion is changed hearts and changed lives. May the light of Tennessee Baptists never be extinguished.

Sometimes, 'Good' is Just Not Good Enough

(Published Jan. 8, 2020)

As December wound to a close, I received word that my great uncle, Blake Wilkey, had died at the age of 98. He was my grandfather's (Pop) last remaining brother. I remembered "Uncle Blake," having visited him many times as a child, but I had not really kept in touch with him other than updates from my Uncle Bill (Pop's son) and Aunt Lynn, who maintained a close relationship over the years.

Still, I felt like I should attend his funeral, so on New Year's Day, my wife Joyce and I make the approximately four-hour trip to Robbinsville, N.C., located in Graham County, which borders Monroe County in southeast Tennessee near Tellico Plains.

Upon arriving to the funeral home I visited with his wife and two children but didn't really know very many others who were in attendance. The standing joke with the Wilkey family is that you can tell a Wilkey man "by his ears" so I saw several folks whom I assumed were distant cousins. In fact, I later discovered that the two pastors who conducted the funeral were relatives.

It was a simple country funeral. Both men were good friends with my late uncle and spoke highly of him and his family.

One of the pastors began his message by saying, "Blake Wilkey was a good man." He then went on in great detail about how he was a good husband, a good father, a good family man, a good church member, and the list went on.

Then, the elderly country pastor clearly communicated the point he was trying to make: No matter how good Blake Wilkey was, he was not good enough to go to heaven, EXCEPT for a decision he made decades ago when he confessed his sins and gave his heart to Jesus Christ and made Him Lord and Savior of his life.

What a great reminder for all Christians as we begin 2020. How many of us know some really "good" people? They may be your neighbors. They could be people you work with or see at the local baseball and football games where your children play. We all know "good" people — people who would give you the shirts off their backs or come over and help you fix the leaking faucet or toilet in your house.

But, are they good enough? If they were to die tomorrow, would they go to heaven? Hopefully, we know, but sadly, many of us do not because we never asked. Christians, and I am guilty, sometimes assume a person's spiritual condition because of how he or she lives his or her life. We don't take the time to ask if they know Jesus.

In Tennessee, it is estimated that four million of Tennessee's more than seven million population are lost, having no relationship with Jesus Christ. I would dare say that thousands upon thousands of those four million lost Tennessee Baptists are "good people." But being good is not enough.

Look out your car window when you drive to church on Sunday. Eight out of 10 of your neighbors will not be in anyone's church on any given Sunday. And, if you conducted a survey, you probably would discover that many of those folks are "good" people, but good is not good enough.

As we enter a new year, make a resolution to really get to know the people you think you know already. Get acquainted with your neighbors and others you are in constant contact with. By doing so, if you ever have the opportunity to attend a funeral one day, you won't have to wonder, Were they "good" enough? You will know because you shared the good news of Jesus Christ with them.

Volunteer Spirit Shown in Amazing Ways

(Published March 18, 2020)

In the early morning hours of March 3, Tennesseans were awakened by tornado sirens across Middle Tennessee. In just a few minutes (though it probably was an eternity to those directly impacted), the storms moved on to another portion of the state.

The tornadoes left behind at least 24 fatalities, massive destruction and lives turned upside down. According to AccuWeather the total damage and economic loss caused by the March 3 tornadoes is estimated between $1.5 billion and $2 billion. That's billion with a "B."

And, after checking out sites throughout Benton, Davidson, Wilson and Putnam counties, that is not as farfetched as it sounds. Hundreds of houses in the affected counties were just piles of rubble after the storms moved through.

Like any disaster, it is more personal when it happens to yourself or someone you love. In this case, we were spared, but our son Daniel and his wife Jill were in their Lebanon home when the tornado hit their house. They were able to hide in a storm shelter so they escaped unhurt, and we will forever be grateful to God.

Their home, however, took a hard hit as did so many others across Middle Tennessee. Unlike many houses, however, their structure was still standing. Trees were down everywhere on their property.

What happened next is nothing short of a miracle and God's grace and mercy.

Volunteers descended on the hardest hit areas within 24 hours, some even sooner if they could get through the downed trees and power lines.

Before week's end, volunteers had cleared our son's property of downed trees and debris and Tennessee Baptist Disaster Relief volunteers had come by and tarped their roof.

Similar stories were repeated all across Middle Tennessee. In many places, volunteers had to be turned away or sent to other locations because there were so many in one location.

I have always been and will always be a staunch advocate of Tennessee Baptist Disaster Relief. And, DR was visible throughout the days following the tornadoes. But, in some cases, volunteers are needed immediately, before DR teams can get the call out to assigned areas.

That was the case in Middle Tennessee. Volunteers were needed immediately to help begin clean up and to take food and water to people who did not have anything. People showed up in droves with loving hearts and willing hands, ready to do whatever was needed. Churches all across Tennessee sent volunteer teams out for several days.

This outbreak of tornadoes has helped me see more clearly that people may not be trained, but they can still serve and serve effectively. We need both untrained and trained volunteers. Tennessee Baptist Disaster Relief, along with Southern Baptist Disaster Relief, has implemented steps that will involve both trained and untrained workers.

In the days ahead, the number of untrained volunteers will decrease as people return to work and those affected return to a "new normal." But there will still be relief work that needs to be done. That is where Tennessee Baptist DR is at its best. One volunteer leader told me that DR is not a sprint, but instead is a marathon. That is so true.

As the marathon gets longer and longer, Tennessee Baptist DR will still be there, and hopefully, there will be others who can volunteer as they can.

Disaster relief is not rocket science. There are some tasks more difficult than others and some that require specific skills. But, what makes Tennessee Baptist and Southern Baptist DR special is not the skills. Rather, it is the heart and compassion of the volunteers.

Tennessee Baptist volunteers are as ready to share the good news of Jesus Christ as they are to cut up a downed tree or recover family treasures from a pile of debris. Getting your earthly home back in order is essential, but nothing is more important than getting your eternal home in order.

Pray for those who were affected by the tornadoes in the days ahead and also for those volunteers who will continue to show God's love to those who need it. To God be the glory!

(One week after their house was badly damaged by the tornado, Daniel and Jill Wilkey returned home with their daughter, Clara Ann, born on March 8. The Wilkey and Pransky families are extremely blessed.)

WILL COVID-19 MAKE YOU REEVALUATE YOUR PRIORITIES?

(Published April 15, 2020)

COVID-19 has turned lives upside down all over the world. Thousands of people have died and thousands have gotten the disease. Thankfully, many have survived and have recovered from the virus.

Millions of people, however, have not gotten the disease but their lives also have changed. Whoever heard of "social distancing" a month ago? The nation's economy was booming four weeks ago. Now, you can't go out to dinner and "sit inside" a restaurant. Businesses have closed — some temporarily, but others have announced they will not reopen.

For many people, the "workplace" has become their home. It's been four weeks since the staff of the Tennessee Baptist Mission Board began working from home and it still is not easy. For the past 46 years I have "gone" to work. Now, I am learning to adjust to working from home and finding that balance that you have to maintain.

The coronavirus has changed our lives forever. I'm confident "this, too, shall pass," but the memories of pandemic will remain vivid. The pandemic has changed our lives in so many ways that we don't even realize all of them yet.

For decades, America has been a nation on the go. We are too busy. Before the coronavirus, how many people spent most of their evenings at home? There was always the next ball game or practice or the next dance recital to go to. For me, it was looking for that next yard sale or estate sale on the weekend. Even church kept us busy with meetings throughout the week and on Sunday evenings.

Busyness became a way of life, a way of coping for people. If you're busy, you don't have time to think about what's important. The coronavirus, for all of the hurt and anguish it has caused, has forced Americans to slow down and examine what really matters.

I daresay most of us, if we are honest, would say that this virus has helped us to eliminate some of the "stuff" that overwhelms us.

Though I felt like I had a good prayer life and spent time with God in His Word, I have realized the time I truly was spending with Him was not adequate. The uncertainty caused by COVID-19 is a stark reminder that we need to be in constant prayer and communication with the God who is in control.

I have discovered that a nice walk during the time I normally would be stuck in traffic has given me a great opportunity to talk with God in His element.

The pandemic also has forced people to listen to others because we really don't have much else to do. I have had more good conversations on the telephone the past few weeks than I've had in decades because I took the time. I've always had the time, but I didn't use it wisely.

Just last week I had a friend who called me out of the blue. I had not heard from him in several months, but he was just "checking" to see how I was. It was another reminder for me that I need to do the same.

Social distancing has made me have a greater appreciation for the time I spend with family and friends. I have been going through grandchildren withdrawal. That's been the hardest thing for me. My two grandsons live in South Carolina. We "see" each other on video calls, but a video can't give you a hug.

My son and his wife recently presented us with our first grand-daughter, Clara. She's only 30 minutes away but we limit how much time we spend with her because of health concerns related to the virus.

Yet, we anticipate the day when the virus has subsided and we can spend all the time we want with those we love.

I admit that the past four weeks have made me rethink how I need to live post coronavirus. Instead of always being on the go, I need to remember the "good old days" of the virus when we focused more on the needs of others, rather than ourselves.

The coronavirus will eventually end, and we will return to "normal," whatever normal is. My prayer is that we don't return to what we were. Instead, we live like the virus is still with us. No, I am not referring to isolation from others. Instead, we need to rely totally on God. He is what will get us through the virus, and He will be there for us when it's over.

AN EXCUSE BAPTISTS CAN NEVER USE AGAIN

(Published May 13, 2020)

"We've never done it that way before."
If Southern Baptists had a national motto, it would be that simple sentence.

I have attended a Baptist church all of my life — and that now spans 62 years. I have heard that Baptist motto all of my life, and sadly, I have used it myself more than once. And, my guess is that most Baptists, if honest with themselves, will admit they also have said, "We've never done it that way before." Oh, I almost forgot. The second part of that motto is, "And, we're not going to start now."

Thanks to COVID-19, the Baptist motto is no longer valid.

In the past two months, Baptists have had to do a lot of things that "we've never done that way before" and they really had no choice. And, guess what? Our churches are still alive and well. By now, some churches have begun meeting again, but still thousands of Baptist churches are still waiting to re-engage with in-person services.

And, what's more, the world has not ended because we have done things we've never done before.

Just think of all the things that we have been doing in recent weeks that "we have never done that way before." Here's just a few:

• We have worshipped together off site. We have listened to our pastors and church musicians either through video or livestream technology. God's Word has been proclaimed. And, more people have heard gospel messages through technology who would never have entered the door of a church.

• We have learned that technology is not necessarily "evil." When we couldn't leave our homes, we could still "see" and fellowship with folks through mediums such as Facebook, Zoom and others. We miss the handshakes and the hugs but technology has enabled us to see each other when we couldn't leave our houses. We have still been able to "attend" Sunday School, prayer sessions and meetings. Unfortunately, even COVID-19 couldn't erase Baptist meetings.

• We have rediscovered the telephone, or at least what the telephone was intended for. With the emergence of Facebook, Twitter, texting and more, conversations were going the way of the dinosaur. COVID-19 has allowed us to actually call our friends and engage in meaningful conversations, instead of exchanging a few words or waving at each other from afar on Sunday mornings. And, while on the topic of speaking, I have talked with more of my neighbors than ever before while taking a walk each day.

• We are more intentional in caring for each other. We have checked on people to see if they had needs that we could meet. COVID-19 has helped us become more aware of the circumstances of those around us. Only God knows how many meals or groceries have been left on porches of people who were at risk for the disease and could not leave their homes.

As we get back to our workplaces, churches and schools, may we not fall back into that trap of thinking we can't try or do new things. We might even discover there are things we used to do that we can do differently and maybe, just maybe, even better than before. Let's not let the lessons learned from COVID-19 go for naught.

---

40 Years — Where Did the Time Go?

(Published Sept. 23, 2020)

Psalm 144:4 (HCSB) reminds us, "Man is like a breath; his days are like a passing shadow."

That verse became real to me this year as I realized that 40 years ago this month, God started me on a journey I never expected. I had my plans, but I soon learned that plans made without God rarely pan out.

When I graduated from the University of South Carolina in

1980 with a journalism degree in hand, I knew I would soon be the Gamecocks beat reporter for the *Greenville News,* but that's not what God had in mind.

I had never actually worked for a newspaper before, though I had articles published while in college, so God led me to the *Northwest Sentinel,* a community newspaper in the upstate. Its mother paper was the established *Pickens Sentinel* in the next county over from where I lived. The editor, Ben Bagwell, wanted someone who lived in the area to serve as news editor. I loved it. He became a mentor and friend and helped me become a better journalist along the way.

But, I soon discovered I would not make much of a living at a small weekly paper. God worked it out by giving me another part-time position at North Greenville College (now University), a Baptist school where I earned my associate's degree while it was still a junior college.

Actually I discovered that two part-time jobs with a newspaper and a small college were barely enough for me to scratch out a living but I loved both positions. God was not through. He later arranged for me to move into full-time Christian ministry by moving me to Baptist College at Charleston (now Charleston Southern University) in public relations and later the Education Commission of the Southern Baptist Convention where I would be involved in communications and edit my first Southern Baptist publication, the *Southern Baptist Educator.*

It was at the Education Commission that I began to write stories for Baptist Press, both as part of my job and during the Southern Baptist Convention annual meetings. Dan Martin, then editor of Baptist Press, was one of the best journalists I have ever known. He taught me the "ins and outs" of the profession.

During that time I came to know a lot of folks who worked at Baptist state papers and I knew that was where God wanted me to be. In 1988, former *B&R* editor William Fletcher Allen hired me as his associate editor and I have been on the staff ever since.

When Fletcher retired in 1998 I wanted to become the editor, but for the most part, the paper did not have a history of promoting from within. But again, God opened door after door and in September of 1998, I was elected as editor of the *B&R*. Looking back, I realize that every position I held prepared me for the next one.

The journey has not always been easy, but God has been with me every step of the way. Criticism has never bothered me that much. Having been a journalist and a baseball umpire gave me a pretty thick skin. The only time I really got upset was when a pastor questioned my salvation once. God took care of that for me and called him to another state.

What has overwhelmed me has been people, who over the years, have told me how much the paper has meant to them. A few weeks ago, I received a text from Joyce Rickman, wife of TBMB staff member and longtime Tennessee pastor Gary Rickman. She asked me to call because Elizabeth Vantrease, her 94-year-old mother, wanted to talk to me about the paper.

I called and we had a wonderful conversation. She basically had read the paper her entire life. She told me how that when she was a child, her mother would read the Bible and the *B&R* on Sunday afternoons to her children and her daddy who could not read. What an incredible testimony.

Joyce later told me that the conversation "made" her mother's day. It also made my day and year for that matter. It was just another confirmation that I never was meant to be a beat writer for the Gamecocks.

I recently read this verse from Psalm 40:5 (CSB) that sums up the past four decades. "Lord, my God, you have done many things. Your wonderful works and plans for us; none can compare with you. If I were to report and speak of them, they are more than can be told."

God has blessed me by allowing me to serve Him and Tennessee
Baptists through the ministry of writing and helping to tell His stories.

OF ALL PEOPLE, CHRISTIANS SHOULD BE THANKFUL

(Published Nov. 18, 2020)

The year 2020 has been one of the most difficult years in the lives of
many Americans.

It has been a year filled with anxiety and fear due to COVID-19,
racial tensions and riots across the country, and one of the most bitter
and contested presidential elections in modern history, if not all time.
Even after a winner has been declared, many people are upset and the
election results probably will be contested in the courts.

And, just remember, no matter how you voted or whether you
liked the election results or not, the sun has risen every day since Nov.
3 and I have no reason to think it won't (unless Jesus returns sooner
than later). God is still on His throne.

As Thanksgiving approaches next week, there are literally countless
people who probably feel they have no reason to be thankful this year.
People have lost loved ones due to COVID. Some lost their jobs. Still,
others have dealt with other illnesses and trials that life brings our way.

In spite of trials and tribulations, we still can be thankful. People
without Christ may not feel that way, but Christians should never get
to that point. As the old hymn reminds us, "Count your blessings,
name them one by one."

Do a quick Google search on your computer and you will find at
least 100 Bible verses that talk about thankfulness.

Here is one that is meaningful to me: 1 Chronicles 16:34 (CSB)

— "Give thanks to the Lord, for He is good; His faithful love endures forever."

As I reflect on this year from the perspective of the Wilkey family, it has been tough but God has blessed in many ways. When a tornado struck Middle Tennessee in March, it severely damaged the home of my son, Daniel, and his wife, Jill, who was almost nine months pregnant, but they were unhurt.

In the aftermath of the storm, dozens upon dozens of volunteers became the hands and feet of Jesus, showing them His love by clearing debris and trees off their home and property.

Then, almost exactly one week later, God gave them and us the blessing of Clara Ann, our first granddaughter. With Clara and our two grandsons in South Carolina (Eli and Parker) we are blessed beyond measure.

We have so many other reasons to give thanks, including the fact that our family has remained relatively healthy in the midst of a worldwide pandemic.

I daresay that every Tennessee Baptist can find multiple reasons to give thanks to God as Thanksgiving Day approaches next week.

I know one reason we all have as Christians, and I left the best for last. John 3:16 (HCSB) gives us the greatest reason why we can be thankful: "For God loved the world in this way: He gave His one and only Son, so that everyone who believes in Him will not perish but have eternal life."

What a promise and what a reason to be thankful!

Among the many blessings we are thankful for in 2020 are our grandchildren: Clara Wilkey, who was born this year, with her cousins, Parker (left) and Eli Beasley.

TRADITIONS MAY BE ALTERED BUT FOCUS REMAINS

(Published Dec. 16, 2020)

Christmas celebrations may look a little different this year for many Tennessee families in 2020 as they deal with the reality of COVID-19.

But take heart. One thing COVID-19 can't affect is the reason we celebrate Christmas — the birth of our Savior, Jesus Christ.

Christmas is always hard on families who have lost loved ones during the year and 2020 will be no different. As of Dec. 6, there were 4,943 reported deaths from COVID in the state, according to www. tn.gov/health.

And though one death from the disease is too many, the state health department reports that more than 340,000 people have recovered from the disease. That is something to be thankful for. I have had several relatives and friends who have recovered from the disease. We rejoice in those recoveries.

But we can't take the disease for granted. Cases continue to spike and as of today, the vaccine is not ready for distribution. COVID-19 is still rampant and it is imperative we take precautions.

Many Tennessee Baptist churches have foregone live Christmas musicals and presentations this year. Still, some churches have found unique ways to still celebrate the birth of our Savior.

For those who could not attend a live performance or even watch one virtually, you can still celebrate the birth of our Savior. Sing your own carols, either as a family or individually. While driving down the road, turn off the radio and sing those beautiful carols such as "Silent Night," "Away In a Manger" and "Joy to the World."

And, as families gather for Christmas celebrations, many are taking precautions, not out of fear but out of love for family members who have health issues that may make them susceptible to the disease.

My family is no exception. For nearly 20 years, my immediate family has celebrated Christmas with my Uncle Bill, Aunt Lynn and their three children and their families in South Carolina. We traditionally have met in my aunt and uncle's home or occasionally at one of my cousins' home. This year, however, we will not be able to hold our annual gathering. My uncle has some serious health issues and our entire family wants to make sure he is protected.

We originally planned to social distance as individual families and wear masks except when eating. Is it something we wanted to do? Of course not. But this is not a "normal" year. Last week, as cases continued to spike in South Carolina, we decided the best thing was to cancel this year. Was it an easy decision? Actually it was. Protecting someone we love dearly took precedence over tradition.

While we can't gather as extended family, I'm sure we will all gather with our individual families. That's our plan for now. And while my aunt and uncle can't be with us, we will continue a tradition they were doing when we first started sharing Christmas with them over 20 years ago. A family member will read the Christmas story on Christmas Eve. That is one tradition we can keep and treasure.

Other families will face similar decisions. A recent survey of Americans by Lifeway Research indicate about 35 percent of those surveyed planned to visit less with family this year. COVID-19 is real and families need to consider what's best for all concerned.

The important thing is to not focus on what you can't do. Focus on what you can do. So, if your family does have to alter a time-honored tradition this year, don't get discouraged. Observe whatever traditions you can and change some others for the good of everyone. Whatever you do, keep the focus on Jesus. After all, He is "the reason for the season."

(My last remaining uncle, Bill Wilkey, died less than two weeks after Christmas on Jan. 4, 2021 at the age of 83. He was more than an uncle. See "Remember America's heroes — our veterans," published Nov. 2, 2016.)

Don't Let the World Rob You of Your Joy

(Published March 16, 2022)

Suffice to say, our world is in a mess.

COVID-19 is beginning its third year and has shown no sign of going away. People are still catching the disease and, sadly, some are still dying.

Russia has invaded the Ukraine. Thousands of people have died and people are fleeing the country.

Gas prices are skyrocketing. In Tennessee, gas has exceeded $4 a gallon in some places and it is knocking on the door at other gas stations. I got a bargain last week, $3.79 a gallon.

Time magazine reported in January of this year that the number of violent crimes is on the rise in the nation. Homicides rose nationally by 7 percent in 2021, according to *Time.*

The list can go on and on. We all know families who have been affected adversely because of the pandemic. Some folks lost their jobs and while there are plenty of jobs available, especially in the restaurant business, many families struggle to make ends meet.

It's easy to get caught up in the hopelessness we see in our world.

Christians have a distinct advantage over non-Christians when the world appears to be falling apart. We have hope that can be found only in Jesus Christ. Unfortunately, too many Christians get caught in the trap/sin of worry. My grandmother was one of the most godly women I have ever known. She was instrumental in leading me to Christ, but that woman could have written a book on how to worry. If there was a Ph.D. available for worriers, Mom would have graduated with honors. She read her Bible and had tremendous faith, but she still worried. We use to tease her that she would worry about not having anything to worry about.

The Bible, however, makes it clear that worrying is a waste of time and that it keeps us from doing what really matters — sharing the love of Jesus Christ with others. I try to remind myself of this often because I think I inherited my grandmother's tendency to worry. There are many excellent passages in Scripture, especially Matthew 6:25-34 (CSB). Verse 25 states it clearly, "Don't worry about your life ... . Then verse 34 ends the passage with this reminder, "Therefore don't worry about tomorrow because tomorrow will worry about itself. Each day has enough trouble of its own."

And, Philippians 4:6 (CSB) also makes it plain, "Don't worry about anything, but in everything, through prayer and petition with thanksgiving, present your requests to God."

We all have times when we are down and we let life's circumstances weigh us down. But do we stay that way or do we trust God to deliver us from worry? It's all about attitude. We can live life with a dour look all the time or we can let the joy of Jesus shine brightly. Ultimately, it's up to us.

My wife and I recently stayed at a hotel and we met the lady who checked us in. She had an infectious attitude and she loved to talk. She shared that she held three jobs, but she radiated joy, not self-pity. She was doing what she needed to take care of herself and her family. She could have been bitter and depressed, but her attitude did not reflect those traits. Other guests came in so we did not get to have a gospel conversation, but I have a strong sense that she was a woman of faith.

What do people see when they look at us? Do they see Jesus or do they see someone who appears hopeless and depressed.

It's not easy, but we can't let the circumstances of the world rob us of the joy of the Lord and the hope that can only be found in Him. After all, it's that hope in Jesus that carries us through the worst of times. As He reminds us in John 16:33 (NIV), "In the world you will have tribulation, but take courage, I have overcome the world."

EVERYONE NEEDS A 'BOOTSIE' AND A 'SHIRLEY'

(Published May 25, 2022)

Bootsie Coggins died on Mother's Day.

Very few people in Tennessee know who Edward "Bootsie" Coggins is. But in heaven and northern Greenville County in South Carolina, Bootsie Coggins is a spiritual giant, even though he was about five feet, four inches tall and a hundred pounds or so soaking wet.

Other than my grandparents and my Aunt Lynn and Uncle Bill, no one played a more major role in my spiritual development other than Bootsie and his wife, Shirley. To mention one without the other is impossible. Married for more than 63 years, they went together like cobbler and ice cream. I was blessed to be an "honorary" member of their family which included their children, Randy and Lavonda.

Bootsie had a tough home life growing up. His dad was a bootlegger, thus his nickname. He would be the first to admit he was not a good person in his teenage years and early adulthood.

Even after he married Shirley, a strong Christian woman, he ran from religion. He told stories of hiding in the bedroom when the preacher would come to visit. But he soon discovered he might run, but he could not hide from God. Bootsie eventually gave his life to God and, in doing so, countless lives would be impacted over the next 50-plus years.

When Bootsie became a Christian, "old things" passed away. He was a new creation, and he lived like it. Bootsie gave his life not only to God but to Lima Baptist Church, a small rural congregation in Travelers Rest, S.C., not too far from the North Carolina line.

Bootsie did everything at Lima but preach and he could have done that. He was especially adept at preaching to Randy and me on the occasions we needed it, and they were more often than not. I spent more time at their house than I did mine in my teenage and early adult years.

I daresay there is not a young person who spent time at Lima who was not impacted by Bootsie and Shirley. They never had the title but for all practical purposes, they were the unofficial youth leaders at Lima. They would load us up and take us to a state park to swim and have picnics and to countless other places. They invested their lives in the children and youth at Lima. Among other things, Shirley led the youth choir and Bootsie led the RAs.

A group would gather at their house on Sunday nights for her famous corn bread and onions and her pound cake and other desserts. They loved Jesus, and they showed that love to all of us.

But, Bootsie impacted more than just the youth. He taught an adult Sunday School class for 40 years and served as a deacon for decades. Lima was a small country church and could never attract established pastors other than retirees who would serve at the end of their ministry. Most of our pastors were just beginning their ministry and as a result, had to "learn on the job." Bootsie became a mentor and friend to so many pastors who acknowledged his impact on them and their ministry. Two of them spoke at his funeral.

I would not be the person I am today had Bootsie and Shirley Coggins not been in my life. They didn't just talk about Jesus. They modeled what it meant to be a Christian. They also modeled what it meant to have a Christian home and to live by faith.

I had the privilege of speaking at Lima's homecoming last year and Bootsie and Shirley, who both had health issues in recent years, were able to be there. That's a memory I won't soon forget. We will all miss Bootsie, but we know where he is. There is no doubt in my mind that he heard a booming, "Well done my good and faithful servant" when he stepped through the Pearly Gates.

Bootsie and Shirley are examples of countless faithful Christians who serve the Lord they love without any fanfare. Our Tennessee churches are full of "Bootsies and Shirleys" who have impacted countless lives because they were lives who were changed by God.

My prayer is that my wife and I can be a "Bootsie and Shirley" to someone. I hope that will be your prayer as well.

TRUST GOD, NOT GPS

(Published Jan. 25, 2023)

Two weeks ago I traveled to southeastern Kentucky to provide news coverage of rebuilding efforts from flooding which hit that region last summer.

I was in Newport, so I plugged in the address in my phone's GPS and off I went.

For this particular destination, my GPS took me up through Tazewell, into Harrogate and across the state line into Kentucky. Normally, when I am on the road I am supposed to be, I check the mileage to the next turn off and the name of the road. Unfortunately, I neglected to follow my usual routine.

After several miles of winding through the mountain roads of Kentucky, I lost my GPS signal. At first, no big deal. That happens often when traveling. But as I traveled on, it didn't come back. I still wasn't too concerned. I knew I was heading in the general direction.

I decided to call Stanley Roach, disaster relief director for the Knox County Baptist Association who was leading efforts helping residents near Carrie, Ky., with repairing their homes. I knew he could guide me in. But, when I called him, there was no signal. Imagine that.

So, there I was in the middle of the mountains of Kentucky, basically lost, not knowing where I was going.

I learned two valuable lessons on that three-plus hour trip to southeastern Kentucky. First, I should have printed out my directions ahead of time. Then, it would not have mattered when technology failed me.

Second, you don't need technology to communicate with God. Prayer works no matter where you are. I prayed as I drove that God would guide me in the right direction. After driving for miles, I finally found a gas station. I must admit, the gas station attendant was not much help. She had never heard of my destination, but she "sort of know" the direction I needed to go.

I set off again, determined to find my way. As I kept driving, I saw a sign noting that I was leaving the Daniel Boone National Forest. That was how lost I was. I didn't even know I was in the national forest.

Long story short, I finally got to where I was going. And, believe it or not, the distance was exactly the same as my GPS had indicated it would be when I started. Now, it might not have been exactly the same route, but I know God led me through those mountains.

As I have pondered that experience, I knew I was lost, but I also knew who would rescue me from being lost.

Not everyone has that luxury and assurance. According to most statistics, about four million people live in Tennessee and nearly two-thirds of the population are lost because they do not know Jesus Christ as their personal Lord and Savior.

Sadly, a large number of those people probably know they are lost and don't care. They do not think that they need a Savior.

Even sadder are the millions of people who live in our state who are lost and don't even know it.

And, what's more, they may never know unless we, as Tennessee Baptists, tell them.

Think about it. On any given day, two out of every three people you pass are probably on the road to hell. Do we care?

I think and pray that we do. Be intentional this year. While not everyone is comfortable sharing the gospel one on one, we can all invite people to church. Sometimes, an invitation is all that is needed to see someone set on the road to being baptized and discipled.

All of us who have professed Jesus as Lord and Savior know what it's like to be lost. It's a horrible feeling. Let's all do our part to decrease the lostness in Tennessee in 2023.

And, do you know the best part about sharing Jesus? You don't need technology. Technology will fail, but trust in Jesus will help you in any situation, including sharing the gospel with someone who truly is lost.

PASSAGE OF TIME CHANGES PERSPECTIVE

(Published July 5, 2023)

Most all of my mother's side of the family grew up in Graham County, N.C., near the small town of Robbinsville.

Today, Robbinsville is a tourist attraction noted for the beauty of its mountains and outdoor life and its proximity to the Cherohala Skyway, a scenic mountain highway, and the Tail of the Dragon, an 11-mile stretch of road from Tennessee into Graham County used by motorcycles and sports cars. The road is known for its 318 curves.

Nearly 60 years ago, none of that mattered to a young boy who had to "endure" a three or four hour trip (it seemed like days) to visit relatives in Robbinsville. Today, with better roads, the trip is slightly over two hours.

As far as I was concerned, Robbinsville was the "uttermost" end of the earth as described in Scripture.

And, it didn't get much better once we arrived. Don't get me wrong. I loved my great grandparents and aunts and uncles that we always visited. We were treated and fed extremely well. Most of them did not have television, or if they did, I never watched anything there.

For a boy from age 5 through 9 or so, it truly seemed like Robbinsville was in the middle of nowhere.

Yet, as I look back, I do remember playing in the creek across from one of my great uncles' house and the family reunions that were held regularly.

It didn't mean much then, but now at age 65, I have a different perspective. Those memories and days gone by are now so much more important to me now than when they occurred.

My great grandparents, my grandfather and his three brothers are now gone and in heaven but in June of this year, the siblings of his family arranged for a reunion at my great uncle's house. His wife, Helen Louise, now in her 90s is the only remaining member of that generation. She and her children, Rachel and Sidney, opened up their property to more than 100 descendants of Frank and Bessie Wilkey, my great grandparents.

My entire family, including my son and daughter and their spouses and children, made the trek to Robbinsville.

Some of us rented a cabin less than a mile from where my great grandparents' house still stands.

I can't help but note the irony. I paid money to return to the place I dreaded going to as a child. What's more it was more than worth what we paid.

Our grandkids played in the same creek I played in as a kid. They had a blast.

The reunion was great as well, and I reconnected with relatives I had not seen in years. It was a wonderful time of fellowship, fun and amazing food.

While there, we also visited one of my mother's first cousins (Lavina) on her mother's side of the family and had a great time. She had some amazing pictures of my grandmother (Mom) and her siblings. Lavina and her husband, Sherman, made us feel so welcomed. Sherman is an amazing woodworker and he gave my grandsons puzzles of the whale that swallowed Jonah (yes, I know the Bible describes it as a big fish) but he made what is commonly accepted. Take the puzzle apart and Jonah is actually inside. It was an amazing piece of craftsmanship.

The three-day trip was an incredible journey down memory lane. It was almost as if I could hear my grandparents laughing at how much I enjoyed the trip, remembering how much I complained about having to go when I was a kid.

Our roots are important. Who we are today is dependent a great deal on those who have gone before us.

Robbinsville is not only the place of my physical roots, it is where my spiritual roots began as well. My grandparents, especially my grandmother, were influential in me coming to know Christ as my Lord and Savior.

God blessed me with my earthly ancestors, and I know one day I will be reunited with them in heaven along with so many I don't even know. Once we accept Christ, we become a part of the larger family of God. What a reunion that will be.

Grandson Parker Beasley magnet fishes in the creek where I played when I was a boy, across from the house where my great-grandparents lived in Robbinsville, N.C.

JESUS IS THE ONLY 'G.O.A.T'

(Published April 17, 2024)

I remember "the good ole days" when a goat was simply that — an animal, one of God's creations.

I can recall the first time I heard a human referred to as a goat. It occurred during a sports talk show on the radio. I actually thought that the person who called someone a goat was going to get in serious trouble for disrespecting another human being.

I finally realized they were referring to the acronym "G.O.A.T." for "Greatest Of All Time." That is how naïve I was.

The recently concluded women's NCAA basketball season and tournament has brought a renewed focus on "G.O.A.T.," as it relates to Caitlin Clark, a basketball star for the University of Iowa who set the record this year for most points ever scored by a college basketball player.

Iowa lost in the national championship last week to my South Carolina Gamecocks, who also have had players in the past who could make a claim for G.O.A.T. status. Dawn Staley, the South Carolina coach, paid tribute to Clark for her contributions to women's basketball during her postgame comments and even referred to her as a G.O.A.T.

But is she? Is anyone for that matter? Maybe, but only if you qualify a specific category such as women's basketball player — and even then, it is impossible.

Think of all people you have heard of who have been referred to as a G.O.A.T. — Tom Brady and Patrick Mahomes (football), Michael Jordan, Labron James, Kobe Bryant (basketball), and the lists go on for all sports.

Who I might consider the greatest baseball player of all time will differ greatly with a 25-year-old today. My answer would be players like Willie Mays and Hank Aaron and pitchers like Tom Seaver, Bob Gibson or Sandy Kofax. Today's generation would have a list totally different from mine.

That is why it is so hard to define who is the greatest person in any area of life — sports, business, singers, actors, etc. The list is endless. It is a matter of individual perspective and choice and it depends on the era in which you live. The bottom line is that only one person can ultimately be the greatest.

Take Clark for instance. She is certainly one of the all-time great women basketball players of this era, but there are many people who do not like her for whatever reason and discount what she has done. She broke a record set by Pete Maravich in the 1970s, and people said you can't compare the two because he did not play with a three-point line or shot clock (which is true). But, you can't discount what Caitlin Clark has done. She is an excellent basketball player. But some comments about her on X (formerly Twitter) after the national championship game were vitriolic. That is sad and unfair.

To debate the issue on who is the greatest in any walk of life is senseless and a waste of time.

Only one person who has ever walked this earth deserves to be called the "G.O.A.T." and that is Jesus Christ, the son of God who knew no sin. Jesus transcends time. He is the Alpha and the Omega, the beginning and the end.

Jesus gave His life so that sinners (and that includes everyone) can have eternal life if we confess our sins, repent and trust in Him for salvation. No one else even comes close.

So, unless you are referring to Jesus Christ, stop using the words "greatest or G.O.A.T." The world has had a lot of great people in its history and will continue to have more, but **only** Jesus can be described as the greatest.

Printed in the USA
CPSIA information can be obtained
at www.ICGtesting.com
LVHW010603010924
789687LV00003B/6